DISCARD

CONTENTS

FOREWORD

Young people today are bombarded with information. Aside from traditional sources such as newspapers, television, and the radio, they are inundated with a nearly continuous stream of data from electronic media. They send and receive e-mails and instant messages, read and write online "blogs," participate in chat rooms and forums, and surf the Web for hours. This trend is likely to continue. As Patricia Senn Breivik, the dean of university libraries at Wayne State University in Detroit, states, "Information overload will only increase in the future. By 2020, for example, the available body of information is expected to double every 73 days! How will these students find the information they need in this coming tidal wave of information?"

Ironically, this overabundance of information can actually impede efforts to understand complex issues. Whether the topic is abortion, the death penalty, gay rights, or obesity, the deluge of fact and opinion that floods the print and electronic media is overwhelming. The news media report the results of polls and studies that contradict one another. Cable news shows, talk radio programs, and newspaper editorials promote narrow viewpoints and omit facts that challenge their own political biases. The World Wide Web is an electronic minefield where legitimate scholars compete with the postings of ordinary citizens who may or may not be well-informed or capable of reasoned argument. At times, strongly worded testimonials and opinion pieces both in print and electronic media are presented as factual accounts.

Conflicting quotes and statistics can confuse even the most diligent researchers. A good example of this is the question of whether or not the death penalty deters crime. For instance, one study found that murders decreased by nearly one-third when the death penalty was reinstated in New York in 1995.

Death penalty supporters cite this finding to support their argument that the existence of the death penalty deters criminals from committing murder. However, another study found that states without the death penalty have murder rates below the national average. This study is cited by opponents of capital punishment, who reject the claim that the death penalty deters murder. Students need context and clear, informed discussion if they are to think critically and make informed decisions.

The Hot Topics series is designed to help young people wade through the glut of fact, opinion, and rhetoric so that they can think critically about controversial issues. Only by reading and thinking critically will they be able to formulate a viewpoint that is not simply the parroted views of others. Each volume of the series focuses on one of today's most pressing social issues and provides a balanced overview of the topic. Carefully crafted narrative, fully documented primary and secondary source quotes, informative sidebars, and study questions all provide excellent starting points for research and discussion. Full-color photographs and charts enhance all volumes in the series. With its many useful features, the Hot Topics series is a valuable resource for young people struggling to understand the pressing issues of the modern era.

INTRODUCTION

Homosexuality is defined as sexual attraction to a person of the same sex. Although no one argues with the definition, opinions vary widely about whether this attraction is natural, originating in a person's biology, or whether it is a lifestyle choice. To some, it does not matter. But to others, this argument is central to the question of how far society is obligated to go to promote equal rights for homosexuals and protect them from discrimination. The arguments become even more complicated and emotional when children are involved. Thousands of gay families, headed by both men and women, have children. Moreover, gay and lesbian children and teenagers, of both heterosexual and homosexual parents, have difficulty learning in school if they do not feel safe.

Since the 1960s, gays and lesbians have become an increasingly visible presence, and their demands for equal rights more outspoken. Legislators in every state in the country, as well as the federal government, have labored to balance the opposing views of those who favor gay rights and those who feel that homosexuality is immoral and should not be recognized with special considerations. In the thick of the battle, businesses have offered rights to gay employees to cultivate their markets, to keep up with gay rights legislation, and to remain competitive. It is still not clear how the battle for gay rights will end. Someday gay rights might seem like an antiquated idea that reached its heyday in the early 2000s and burned out; or a day could come when people find it hard to believe that gays had to fight for the same rights as other citizens.

Gays and lesbians are increasingly visible these days. Here, Karson Kressley of the popular television series Queer Eye for the Straight Guy participates in a parade celebrating gays and lesbians.

A New Civil Rights Movement

Although gay rights have figured prominently in the news in recent years, homosexuality itself is not new. The earliest recorded history of humans documents examples of same-sex attraction. What has changed, however, is the visibility of gays and lesbians at every level of society and the development of an active and vocal gay community. That community's insistence that its members deserve both recognition and fair and equal treatment under the law has gained enormous strength in the past fifty years. The increasing visibility of the gay community has also motivated an equally strident opposition to gay rights. Many people argue that gay citizens do not need or deserve rights that they believe to be above and beyond rights accorded to all American citizens.

The arguments on both sides of this issue revolve around the question of whether homosexuality is a choice. Gay rights activists claim that homosexuality is an inborn genetic trait, which is determined at the moment of conception. While scientists have not yet identified a gene for homosexuality, gays and lesbians insist that from the time they are small children, they are aware that their sexuality differs from that of most people around them. Gay rights opponents argue just as vehemently that homosexuality cannot be natural, since the human species, like all species, is designed by nature to reproduce. Since same-sex partners cannot have children on their own, this argument follows, homosexuality cannot be natural. Furthermore, many people believe that homosexuality is a disorder that can be cured and, therefore, should be treated by doctors and mental health professionals rather than encouraged and accepted by the government.

Homosexuality in the Nineteenth Century

Today's gay rights movement in the United States can best be understood in the context of the country's social history as a whole. Through the eighteenth and nineteenth centuries, homosexuals were considered insane and treated the same way as other mental patients. They were often locked up in insane asylums for long periods. Sometimes their sex organs were removed. Opinions varied greatly then, as they do now, about whether homosexuality was acquired during childhood or adolescence, or was an inborn trait like eye or hair color. Regardless, the consequences of being identified as a homosexual were so severe that most homosexuals kept their orientation well hidden.

In this detail from an ancient Roman tomb painting, two men recline on a couch as they embrace each other.

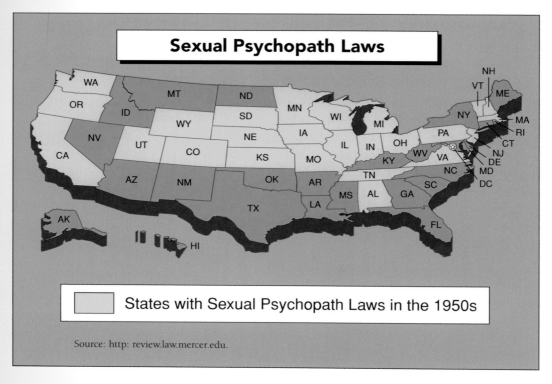

Sexual Psychopath Laws

☐ States with Sexual Psychopath Laws in the 1950s

Source: http: review.law.mercer.edu.

The necessity of hiding one's sexual orientation to avoid punishment and shame began to change as American society became more industrialized and increasingly mobile. Children no longer necessarily settled down in the same small towns where they had been born and raised. This made it easier for young people to hide their personal lives from their families. Then World War I and, later, World War II dispersed young people even farther and wider. This newfound independence had a great effect on young gay and lesbian adults, who were no longer as constrained by fear of the opinions of their family or neighbors who had known them all their lives. Gay and lesbian communities developed in the cities, giving gays and lesbians both strength in numbers and increasing visibility.

This increased visibility provoked a backlash. Many people viewed homosexuality as a threat to traditional families because the homosexual lifestyle conflicted with what they believed to be the fundamental purpose of marriage—to bear children. As a result, laws were passed to punish homosexuality. After World War II, more than half of the states in the United States passed laws explicitly banning what they termed sexual psychopaths. Male homosexuals were the primary target of those laws. In the late 1950s, the district attorney in Sioux City, Iowa, for example, used these laws to commit twenty-nine male homosexuals to insane asylums. There were no time limits on these sentences. Homosexuals could be locked up for the rest of their lives. Many were.

World War II had another effect on the evolution of gay rights. In the 1940s, German and Austrian psychoanalysts dominated the field of psychiatry in both this country and Western Europe. They believed that homosexuality was a disorder resulting from a person's unconscious conflicts resulting from an overbearing mother and a father who was either physically or emotionally absent from a child's life. They also believed that homosexuality could be cured. When many of these psychoanalysts immigrated to the United States during and after the war, their view that homosexuality was a curable mental disorder became the guiding principle for psychiatrists in this country.

Belief in a "Cure" for Homosexuality

Among the most influential psychoanalysts were Irving Bieber and Charles Socarides, both frequent speakers at annual meetings of the American Psychiatric Association (APA) and contributors to respected medical journals. Both Bieber and Socarides were considered leaders in the field of psychiatry, and they believed that homosexuality could be cured. By the late 1960s, the ideas of these two psychoanalysts and their recommendations for the treatment of homosexuality had become standard practice in psychiatry. In his book *Cures*, Martin Duberman relates Socarides' message to the American Medical Association's (AMA's) annual meeting in San Francisco in 1968: "Socarides spoke of homosexuality as a 'dread dysfunction, malignant in character, which has risen to epidemic proportions,' and he called on the federal government to establish centers for the 'cure' of these dangerous creatures."[1] With proper therapy, both Socarides and Bieber insisted, homosexuals could be transformed into heterosexuals.

Their recommendations included intensive talk therapy, treatment with male hormones, and even aversion therapy, in which patients were shown pornography and then electrically shocked or forced to vomit. Socarides claimed a 50 percent cure rate with patients who were treated with talk therapy four or five times a week. Electroshock treatment was reserved for the most difficult and resistant cases.

The Sixties Give Rise to Gay Activism

After decades of oppression and subjection to harsh cures, homosexuals began to fight back in the late 1960s, a decade of general social unrest and dissension. At this time, the nation was deeply divided over the Vietnam War, racial conflicts, and the role of women in public life. Public protests were common. This atmosphere gave rise to the Stonewall rebellion, the first significant protest by homosexuals against their treatment by police. On June 27, 1969, police raided the Stonewall Inn, a bar on Christopher Street in Greenwich Village, New York, that was regularly patronized by homosexuals. Raids at the Stonewall Inn were not uncommon, but for the first time ever, the patrons fought back. Duberman describes the scene at Stonewall that night: "After the police had loaded arrested patrons into a paddy wagon, the crowd that had gathered in front of Stonewall responded with catcalls—and then suddenly exploded, hurling bottles at the officers, using an uprooted parking meter as a battering ram, blockading some of the police inside the bar, and then torching it. Reinforcements rescued the officers, but the rioting was renewed for four nights running."[2] This demonstration quickly became a symbol of a new phase of activism in the gay rights movement.

FIGHTING BACK

"The first night [of the Stonewall rebellion] was probably the most dramatic and the most meaningful to me. . . . My lover and I were stunned and thrilled to see our own kind talking back, berating the cops, and throwing pennies."

Stephen van Cline, quoted in Stonewall Action Identity League, "Stonewall Riots of 1969," September 1998. http://humanists.net/wasm/sail.html.

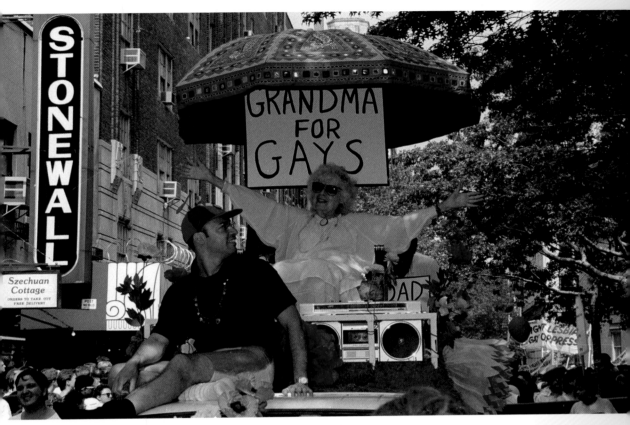

During a gay pride parade, an elderly woman's float rides past the Stonewall Inn, where gay patrons openly resisted police officers during a 1969 raid.

Reported in almost every major newspaper across the country, Stonewall both inspired and focused attention on the increasing militancy of homosexuals. Public protests by gays and lesbians quickly picked up momentum. In 1969, the year the Stonewall rebellion occurred, there were only fifty gay and lesbian organizations with a few thousand members in the entire country. By 1973 the number of organizations had increased to over eight hundred. Gay and lesbian demonstrators often modeled their protests on the civil rights, students', and women's movements. They marched, picketed, and gathered publicly to focus attention on businesses, churches, and government agencies whose policies discriminated against homosexuals.

Targeting the American Psychiatric Association

While the stated purpose of these demonstrations was to campaign for public acceptance and equal treatment under the law, many gays and lesbians viewed such a campaign as highly personal as well. Accustomed to rejection by their families and forced to hide their personal lives from people with whom they worked and interacted every day, gays and lesbians were also desperate for dignity. As Ronald Bayer explains in his book *Homosexuality and American Psychiatry*, "Though not necessarily couched in terms of violence, 'action and rebellion' were seen as antidotes to the shame, self-doubt, and self-hatred that had been imposed upon homosexuals by society."[3] To this end, many homosexual activists believed that it was not enough to selectively target certain organizations with antigay biases. Many gay activists believed that the first thing that had to change was the public perception that homosexuality was abnormal. And, they believed, the most direct route to changing public perception was by changing the definition of homosexuality itself—the definition both created and perpetuated by doctors, which defined homosexuals as mentally ill. The activists believed that effective change must begin within the American Psychiatric Association (APA). Its Diagnostic and Statistical Manual of Mental Disorders (DSM), the guide used to diagnose mental illnesses including homosexuality, was used by every practicing psychiatrist in the country.

Targeting the APA was important for another reason too. Although the number of protests and membership in gay and lesbian organizations had grown significantly, those protests had been wide-ranging and largely unfocused. The new focus on the APA rallied the increasing number of gay protest groups around a common enemy. The field of psychiatry in America began to feel the full force of the frustration and fury of gays and lesbians who were no longer content to accept their status as flawed mentally ill individuals.

This focus on the APA by gay activists coincided with a growing discomfort of a small group of young gay psychiatrists within the APA itself. Unofficially calling itself the "Gay PA," this group met socially each year at the annual meetings of the APA. Not only were they young and gay, but they were also sympathetic with many liberal causes of the day, including students' rights and the anti–Vietnam War movement. One of their goals was to assume more leadership in the APA, whose leaders until that point had been older, more traditional, and politically conservative.

As annual meetings of the APA began to be targeted by gay and lesbian activists outside the organization, the two forces—outside activists and a number of gay psychiatrists on the inside—began a course that gained momentum and resulted in change within three years. In 1970 the annual APA meeting was held in San Francisco, a city with a large gay and lesbian population. One session of that meeting included the screening of a film depicting a cure for male homosexuality that involved gays being forced to vomit at the sight of nude men. Members of the Gay Liberation Front (GLF), a particularly militant pro-gay organization, had secretly gained entrance to the film's showing, and when the nude men appeared on the screen, GLF members cheered and shouted down the psychiatrist who was showing the film.

AN ELABORATE DISGUISE

In the 1970s publicly revealing one's homosexuality could have dire career consequences. Psychiatrist John Fryer announced his own homosexuality but concealed his identity by masquerading as Dr. Anonymous at the American Psychiatric Association meeting in Dallas in 1972. Fryer addressed his fellow psychiatrists wearing a flamboyant multicolored tuxedo that was three sizes too large so that he would appear smaller than he really was. He stretched a large rubber mask of President Richard Nixon over his head, wore a curly wig, and used a voice-distorting microphone. In an account of the incident broadcast by Chicago Public Radio, narrator Alix Spiegel explains: "The disguise was so fantastical that John's own mother would not know him if he sat in her lap."

Alix Spiegel, "81 Words," *This American Life*, episode 204, WBEZ Chicago Public Radio, January 18, 2002.

A LACK OF EVIDENCE

"There is no evidence whatsoever that any child becomes homosexual because he finds an appealing homosexual teacher unless that child is vulnerable and already prepared to go in a homosexual direction."

Judd Marmor, M.D., APA president (1975–1976), quoted in Patricia Saltonstall, "Psyching Out Homosexuality," *Washington Post*, December 18, 1977, p. C1.

The following year, militant gays grabbed microphones and scuffled with psychiatrists who were presenting information about cures for homosexuality. Finally, in 1972 at the APA meeting in Dallas, Texas, the increasing anger of militant gays and the growing discomfort of gay psychiatrists with the APA's definition of homosexuality in the DSM collided. That year, Dr. John Fryer, a psychiatrist who had been fired from the University of Pennsylvania because he was gay, addressed the convention. Fryer, fearing that his career would be ruined if he publicly admitted he was gay, donned an elaborate disguise to hide his identity. Calling himself Dr. Anonymous, Fryer explained how the definition of homosexuality in the DSM had harmed him. He claimed that because homosexuality was defined as a mental illness, he was forced to hide the fact that he was gay from his colleagues and lived in constant fear of losing the career he loved. Fryer's standing ovation both surprised him and reflected the change in attitude that was occurring within the APA.

Then, the next year, Ronald Gold, the media director of the Gay Activists Alliance, convinced Robert Spitzer, a junior member of the APA's committee on nomenclature, to organize a panel discussion at the annual APA meeting in Hawaii. The nomenclature committee is responsible for the wording of every disorder listed in the DSM. Gold, titling his speech "Stop It, You're Making Me Sick," explained to the panel that defining homosexuality as a mental illness in the DSM was "the greatest tool of oppression imaginable."[4] Like Fryer, Gold explained how homosexuals were harmed by being forced to repress their sexuality and pretend to be something they were not. Gold echoed Fryer's contention that homosexuals would never gain full acceptance by society as long as they had to contend with the diagnosis of insanity. Spitzer, convinced by the presentations he heard that day, wrote a resolution to the nomenclature committee suggesting that the definition of homosexuality be changed. He created a new category reserved for homosexuals who either wanted to become heterosexual or who needed help accepting their homosexuality. In other words, he explains, "If you're gay and it doesn't bother you, it can't be considered an illness."[5] The new definition, incorporated into the DSM that fall, was itself short-lived. In December of the same year, mention of homosexuality was omitted from the DSM entirely.

A Turning Point

The change in the DSM had some immediate and very public effects. Every major newspaper featured the story. As Bayer explains,

> Across the country newspapers headlined the American Psychiatric Association's decision. Washington's two major dailies, the *Post* and the *Star* reported, "Doctors Rule Homosexuals Not Abnormal" and "Victory for Homosexuals." The *New York Times* noted in a front-page story, "Psychiatrists in a Shift. Declare Homosexuality No Mental Illness." The gay press exultantly announced the decision in *The Advocate*, declaring "Gays Leave Psychiatric Sick List, and 'Sick No More.'"[6]

The event was a significant turning point that led to many changes in laws and policies regarding homosexuals. In 1974, the year following the decision to change the DSM, the federal Civil Service Commission altered its hiring policy, making it illegal to discriminate against gays and lesbians for most federal jobs. The gay and lesbian community had come out of the so-called closet, which means they had come out of hiding. With the change in the DSM, many people believed that there was no longer any justification for discriminating against gays and lesbians in the military, the government, the workplace, the church, or schools and universities. Within three years of the change, thirty-three cities had changed their statutes to protect the civil rights of gays and lesbians specifically.

Openly gay candidates were elected to local and state offices, including Harvey Milk, who was elected to the San Francisco Board of Supervisors in November 1977.

Even so, opposition to gay rights persisted and even gained strength in some cases. Most of the hiring practices that changed applied to government jobs only. New York City, considered a center of the gay rights movement, repeatedly refused to change its civil rights code to include homosexuals. Teachers' jobs remained at risk if their homosexuality was discovered. Gays and lesbians were still not permitted to become naturalized U.S. citizens if they were born outside the country.

Arguments Against Gay Rights

Although the DSM had changed, public opposition to gay rights was fueled by the belief that the gay and lesbian lifestyle was a threat to traditional family values. Citizens for Community Values (CCV), a conservative Christian group, explains its continuing opposition to gay rights: "One of the primary tenets upon which this organization was established is the Judeo-Christian teaching that the family is the cornerstone of civilization. Inseparably linked to that tenet is the belief that marriage—i.e., one woman and one man living together in a lifelong, monogamous, covenantal relationship—is the foundational element of the family unit."[7] CCV concedes that although some traditions evolve to adapt to the changing needs of society, other traditions—the family structure in particular—cannot change since they are grounded in Scripture, which makes them absolute and eternal.

This belief in the absolute nature of the traditional family helped to garner public support for Anita Bryant's Save Our Children campaign, which began in 1977, the same year that Harvey Milk was elected to the San Francisco Board of Supervisors. Bryant, a pop singer and former beauty queen, led a successful campaign in Florida to repeal a gay rights ordinance that had passed that year in Dade County. She accused gays and lesbians of working to recruit children and turn them into homosexuals. She attracted much media attention as she traveled the country to publicize her success and encourage other cities and counties to follow Dade County's lead.

One objection that was made to drafting laws that protected gays and lesbians from discrimination in the 1970s is still voiced today. Many disputed the necessity for specific laws that protect homosexuals when civil rights laws give legal protection from discrimination to all citizens. Organizations such as CCV argue that laws protecting specifically gays and lesbians are "special rights" that are above and beyond those provided to members of the general population. They explain that view by distinguishing between differences in race or ethnicity, which do deserve protection from discrimination, and differences in behavior, which should not be protected. According to CCV, "Civil rights laws have been enacted in our country to protect classes of people from discrimination based on status—on immutable, distinguishing characteristics that have nothing to do with behavior. A person's race, for example, has nothing to do with that person's lifestyle or behavior patterns. To remove race as a criterion for social decision-making thus makes sense."[8]

In 1977 pop star Anita Bryant addresses the Miami press as she talks about her successful campaign to repeal a gay rights ordinance in Dade County.

CCV argues that society benefits from protecting racial minorities but has nothing to gain by protecting people whose behavior is at odds with accepted lifestyles.

Many others are equally insistent that current laws do not go far enough to protect from discrimination gays and lesbians specifically. Abigail Garner, whose book *Families Like Mine* is a close examination of the issues concerning gay families, argues, "What are labeled as special rights are not special at all; they are human rights that are currently being denied to lesbian and gay citizens."[9] Garner cites job discrimination based on sexual identity, child custody issues that are weighted against gay parents, and the lack of protection of gay students in schools to point out the need for these specific protections.

Being Gay: Is It Something that People Do or Something that People Are?

Part of the reason controversy about gay rights continues is that people still do not agree on whether homosexuality is a behavior or an orientation. Religious Tolerance.org, an organization that represents the views of many religious organizations, explains the varying perspectives:

> Conservative Christians often define homosexuality as something that people do; it is a chosen preference. It is a disorder caused by poor parenting, which can be overcome through therapy and prayer. Gays, lesbians, religious liberals and most therapists believe that homosexuality is something that people are; it is a pre-determined orientation that is normal and natural for them, just as heterosexual orientation is normal and natural for heterosexuals.[10]

But even if someone is born with homosexual inclinations, conservative Christians believe, that person is obligated on moral and religious grounds to avoid homosexual activity.

However, religious conservatives insist that their argument against gay rights does not reflect a bias against homosexual people. They claim their desire to protect gays and lesbians from the destructive homosexual lifestyle is motivated by compassion.

ALWAYS A SIN

Gay rights advocates often argue that homosexuality is an inborn trait and thus should not be considered any more objectionable than heterosexuality. Conservative Christians, however, are unswayed by this view, as self-proclaimed former homosexual Joe Dallas explains:

> For the sake of argument, suppose it could be proven that homosexuality, as a condition, is unchangeable—that no amount of prayer, counseling or efforts of any sort could make a homosexual become attracted to the opposite sex. What then? Should that change our view of homosexual behavior as being sinful? Hardly. There's no contingency in any Scriptural reference to any kind of sin, in the Old or New Testament, saying, Thou shalt not do thus and so—unless, of course, you tried hard to change, went for prayer and counseling, and found you just could not stop wanting to do thus and so. If that's the case, then thus and so is no longer a sin. It's an inborn, immutable gift and you can indulge it!

Joe Dallas, "Responding to Pro-Gay Social Arguments (Part Two)," Focus on the Family, family.org, September 2, 2005. www.family.org/cforum/fosi/homosexuality/theology/a0037786.cfm.

They point to AIDS and other sexually transmitted diseases, the risk of substance abuse, and early death as inherent dangers in the homosexual lifestyle. Many religious groups have established ministries whose goals are specifically intended to reach out to homosexuals and help them overcome their inclinations. Called transformational ministries, these organizations exist across a spectrum of religious groups. Courage, a Roman Catholic ministry, has more than fifteen centers in North America. Evergreen International, a Mormon transformational ministry, was founded in 1989 and devotes its efforts toward overcoming homosexual behavior and diminishing same-sex attraction.

However, some of these transformational ministries have changed their goals since their inceptions. Religious Tolerance.org explains how many transformational ministries now target behavior rather than orientation: "The original goal of most of these ministries was to convert gays and lesbians from having a homosexual orientation into heterosexuals. Increasing numbers of these ministries now realize that such conversions are impossible. They have abandoned attempts to change their clients' sexual orientation, and concentrate on changing behavior."[11] Exodus International is one transformational ministry whose goal

has changed since its founding. If a person makes a conscious choice to avoid same-sex activity, even though his or her orientation remains gay or lesbian, Exodus International considers that person to have been cured of homosexuality.

Religious Tolerance.org lists many other groups and congregations it describes as deeply religious that are supportive and accepting of lesbians and gays and their right to be protected from discrimination. Many of these groups, including the American Friends Service Committee, the United Church of Christ, Presbyterian Church (USA), United Methodist Church, and the American Jewish Congregation, actively promote and lobby for gay rights legislation.

Unanswered Questions Remain

The dispute about whether homosexuality is an inborn trait or a choice has never been fully resolved in the medical community. The APA published a brochure titled *Answers to Your Questions About Sexual Orientation and Homosexuality* that states its belief that homosexuality is a mix of many factors: "Many scientists share the view that sexual orientation is shaped for most people at an early age through complex interactions of biological, psychological, and social factors."[12] The American Medical Association issued a report in 1994 suggesting that psychotherapy be used only to help homosexuals become comfortable with their orientation. The APA goes even further by claiming that it is unethical to attempt to change a person's sexual orientation through therapy. Yet some psychiatrists continue to believe that homosexuality is the result of poor parenting and can be cured. Socarides, the psychoanalyst whose views were challenged by the APA in the early 1970s, attributes the homosexuality of his own son Richard to his failure as a father. Others continue to insist that a person is born to be gay and argue that no one would voluntarily choose a lifestyle that guarantees problems and prejudice. One fact, however, cannot be disputed. The census of 2000 proved that gay men and women live in every state and 99 percent of the counties in the United States. Gays and lesbians have become a strong, vocal, and increasingly visible force.

CHAPTER 2

GAY MARRIAGE

It is traditional in Western culture for heterosexual men and women who love each other and want to raise a family to form permanent, legally binding relationships in the form of marriage. This legal bond is often combined with a religious ceremony so that the couple's commitment to each other is also recognized—or sanctified—by the couple's church, synagogue, or temple. Many people believe that marriages performed by members of the clergy such as priests or rabbis are therefore holy and blessed by God. Once a couple marries, the government then rewards this commitment by giving them legal and financial benefits. Married couples have the option of filing their income taxes together, which can save them money, and they can make legal decisions for each other. In fact, married couples have hundreds of legal advantages over unmarried couples and individuals.

The social and personal advantages of being recognized as a married couple in our society are more difficult to list, but no less important. Others view a married couple as a single unit, more than just two people who love each other. Many private businesses give benefits to married couples in the form of health insurance or even family memberships to health and country clubs. By legalizing their commitment, a couple ensures that their relationship is recognized and respected by every facet of society.

All of this—the legal benefits, the religious recognition, and the social recognition—is at the root of the conflict between those who advocate gay marriage and those who oppose it. Advocates of gay marriage believe that any two committed partners should have the right to marry and gain the benefits of a legal marriage. Opponents believe just as strongly that marriage should be restricted to one man and one woman. Many Americans support adding an amendment to the U.S. Constitution that would limit marriage throughout the country to opposite-sex partners and settle the legal question once and for all.

The Benefits of Marriage

Once the question of gay marriage became a topic of open debate, gay-marriage proponents wanted to know exactly what the benefits of marriage include and what the financial impact is on couples who legally wed. In January 2004 the U.S. General Accounting Office, an agency that reports to Congress, reported that exactly 1,138 federal benefits are granted to married couples. In addition to filing joint tax returns, married couples inherit each other's Social Security and pension benefits when one spouse dies. Married spouses are protected from having to testify against each other in court. If a person is married, it is easier for his or her foreign spouse to immigrate to this country and become a permanent resident or a citizen.

Proponents of gay marriage renew their wedding vows as they stage a marriage equality rally on Capitol Hill in October 2004.

In addition to federal benefits, each state also grants its own benefits to married couples. Greg Moran, a writer for the *San Diego Union-Tribune*, reports, "Experts on sexual orientation estimate that in most states, saying 'I do' confers an additional several hundred state benefits—perhaps as many as 500."[13] In California, state benefits include the ability to make health-care and end-of-life decisions for a spouse. Legally married California couples are eligible for joint home and auto insurance policies and joint rental leases. Married couples are automatically considered joint partners in decisions affecting their children, even if one member of the couple is a nonbiological parent. Married couples can visit each other in the hospital or even in jail as next of kin. These specific benefits granted to couples who marry help motivate the ongoing argument that all couples willing to make a serious commitment to each other should receive the same legal and financial advantages.

Domestic Partnerships and Civil Unions

While many states have passed legislation or amendments to their constitutions that limit marriage specifically to a man and a woman, this has not prevented both those who favor gay marriage and those who oppose it from seeking acceptable alternatives for gay and lesbian couples. In early 2005 California's domestic partnership law went into effect, a law that grants same-sex couples who register as domestic partners virtually all of the legal benefits and responsibilities of married spouses. The Vermont civil union law, which went into effect a few years earlier, also provides gay and lesbian couples with many of the same benefits of marriage, including the right to make medical choices for partners and the ability to file joint state tax returns. However, couples with legal civil unions and domestic partnerships do not take their benefits with them when they cross their state's boundaries. The Defense of Marriage Act, a 1996 federal law defining marriage as a contract between a man and a woman, and a spouse as a member of the opposite sex, gave states the right to refuse to recognize same-sex partnerships licensed in other states.

Though many people view domestic partnerships and civil unions as reasonable alternatives to same-sex marriage, opposition to them comes from both sides of the gay marriage debate.

Gay and lesbian couples argue that the legal status of their relationships should not differ at all from marriages between opposite-sex partners. The Reverend Dr. Troy D. Perry, the first openly gay member of the Los Angeles Human Rights Commission, explains why these alternate arrangements are unsatisfactory: "Civil unions and domestic partnerships do not provide all the legal, economic and social benefits of marriage. They foster a 'separate but equal' status for gays and lesbians—a concept the [Supreme Court] ruled long ago is never equal."[14]

A MATTER OF EQUAL RIGHTS

Advocates of gay marriage often describe the issue as one of fairness that is no different from women seeking the right to vote or African Americans demanding civil rights equal to those of whites. Gay pastor Troy Perry, founder of the Metropolitan Community Church, explains this view:

> Anything less than full marriage equality is second-class status for gays and lesbians. I know the argument: "Can't we get most of our rights through civil unions? Or domestic partnerships? Can't we settle for something less than full marriage equality and still make progress?" Those weren't acceptable answers to women who worked for full legal equality at the turn of the 19th century. Those weren't acceptable answers to African-Americans who worked for full legal equality in the 1950s and 1960s. And they aren't acceptable answers to the lesbian and gay communities who are working for legal equality—including marriage equality—at the dawn of this new millennium.
>
> I have grown weary of the voices that counsel, "Legal change takes time. Be patient." The truth is that the greatest changes in American society have come from bold political strokes. Not incremental change. Think of the Emancipation Proclamation, the Civil Rights Act, and the Americans with Disabilities Act. Incremental? No. Bold? Yes.

Troy Perry, "Why I Believe in Marriage Equality," *San Diego Union-Tribune*, March 14, 2004, p. G4.

Opponents of gay marriage likewise take a dim view of legal contracts between same-sex partners that confer many of the same benefits as marriage. They believe that changing the name of these relationships to domestic partnerships or civil unions simply masks the real agenda of gay activists, who are seeking legal and social approval for gay marriage. Robert Benne and Gerald McDermott, writing for the conservative publication *Christianity Today*, make that point: "The concept of marriage necessarily includes the idea of a man and woman committing themselves to each other. Any other arrangement contradicts the basic definition. Advocates of gay marriage recognize this contradiction by proposing 'gay unions' instead, but this distinction is,

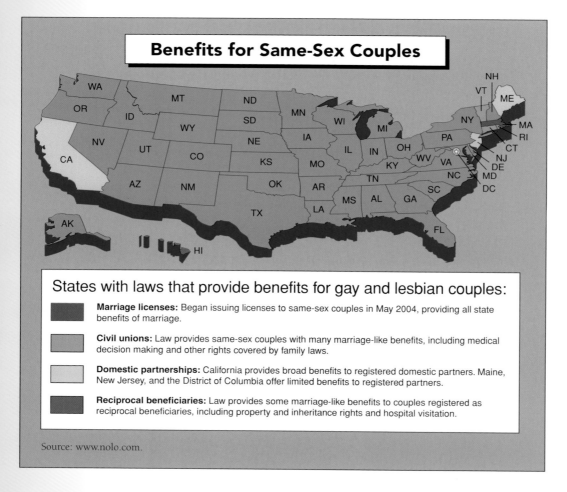

Benefits for Same-Sex Couples

States with laws that provide benefits for gay and lesbian couples:

Marriage licenses: Began issuing licenses to same-sex couples in May 2004, providing all state benefits of marriage.

Civil unions: Law provides same-sex couples with many marriage-like benefits, including medical decision making and other rights covered by family laws.

Domestic partnerships: California provides broad benefits to registered domestic partners. Maine, New Jersey, and the District of Columbia offer limited benefits to registered partners.

Reciprocal beneficiaries: Law provides some marriage-like benefits to couples registered as reciprocal beneficiaries, including property and inheritance rights and hospital visitation.

Source: www.nolo.com.

we believe, a strategic one. The ultimate goal for them is the societal acceptance of gay marriage."[15] Opponents of gay marriage take issue with granting any state-approved benefits to gay couples. They claim that calling these relationships domestic partnerships or civil unions does not change the reality that the state is financing and giving official legal approval to relationships that they believe are fundamentally wrong. They also raise an alarm by claiming that changing the definition of marriage could be extended to demands for state approval of other nontraditional marriages such as bigamy—marriage between one man and two or more women—or even group marriage.

PROTECTING THE COMMON GOOD

"Same-sex 'marriage,' like abortion, contraception and euthanasia, is contrary to the natural law, and thus should be prohibited by the government, whose main duty is to protect the common good."

Matt C. Abbott, letter to the editor, *New York Times*, May 19, 2004, p. A26.

This argument—that once gay partners are allowed to marry, other legal limits on marriage partners will be difficult to defend—is countered by Jonathan Rauch, author of *Gay Marriage: Why It Is Good for Gays, Good for Straights, and Good for America*. Rauch explains, "Gay people are not asking for the legal right to marry anybody they love or everybody they love. That would indeed be a radical transformation of the boundary of marriage, or really an erasure of the boundary altogether. Instead, homosexuals are asking for what all heterosexuals possess already: the legal right to marry somebody they love."[16] Rauch and many other gay marriage advocates believe that opponents to gay marriage purposefully alarm the public with dire warnings that once gay marriage is permitted, people will be able to marry anyone or anything, including their pets.

The Purpose of Marriage

Discussions about legal and financial benefits of marriage and the function of domestic partnerships and civil unions raise an even greater question: Just what is the purpose of marriage itself?

In a San Francisco courtroom in 2004, an opponent of gay marriage holds up a sign encouraging a yes vote on a local proposition that would outlaw same-sex marriage.

Those who oppose gay marriage believe that the fundamental purpose of marriage is to preserve society. At the heart of social preservation they argue, is the traditional family—a mother, a father, and their natural or adopted children. It is in the government's interest, therefore, to encourage people to marry and raise families. The government does this by granting married couples certain benefits that provide the financial security that enables families to afford to have children. Those children, in turn, ultimately support the government, keep society growing and healthy, and move it forward. It follows, then, that the government has no legitimate interest in granting benefits to gay couples since these relationships cannot result in the natural birth of children. This idea is challenged by gay-marriage advocates, who point out that the government supports all heterosexual marriages whether or not the couple is capable or even desirous of having children.

This issue came up in 2005 when San Francisco Superior Court judge Richard Kramer delivered a decision that overturned a ballot measure—Proposition 22—that was approved by 61 percent of California voters in 2000. That ballot measure—also known as the California Defense of Marriage Act—declared that the only valid form of marriage in California was between a man and a woman. In response to the argument of Proposition 22 supporters that procreation is the purpose of marriage, Judge Kramer writes, "One does not have to be married in order to procreate, nor does one have to procreate in order to be married."[17] His opinion reflects the view of many gay-marriage advocates who point to opposite-sex couples such as older couples, who never intend to have children. The government does not require a promise to procreate in order to issue a marriage license.

Those who argue in favor of gay marriage believe that marriage serves an even greater purpose in society. Rauch points out that once a couple has married, spouses are expected to take care of each other for the rest of their lives. Rauch explains, "If I had to pare marriage to its essential core, I would say that marriage is two people's lifelong commitment, recognized by law and society, to care for each other. To get married is to put yourself in another person's hands, and to promise to take that person into your hands, and to do so with a community which expects both of you to keep your word."[18] Married couples care for each other when one spouse becomes ill or incapacitated. This expectation relieves society in general of the burden and responsibility of caring for millions of people. He argues that society would benefit from gay marriage because it would then be able to depend on millions of married homosexuals, in addition to married heterosexuals, to bear these financial and emotional burdens.

> ## GAYS NEXT DOOR
>
> "If the gay couple next door wants to marry, that's fine with me. This world needs all the outward expressions of love that it can get. My marriage is not threatened or devalued in any way, shape, or form."
>
> Jim Land, letter to the editor, *San Diego Union-Tribune*, January 5, 2005, p. B9.

If being married is a stabilizing influence on straight people, as many advocates of gay marriage believe, then society would benefit greatly from supporting its gay citizens in this way too.

While those who support gay marriage argue that it will benefit society, opponents still often voice concern that gay marriage will damage society. To support this view, they point to the 1960s, when social trends changed and couples began living together without being married. Benne and McDermott outline the results of those changes:

> Think back to the 1960s, when illegitimacy and cohabitation were relatively rare. At that time many asked how one young woman having a baby out of wedlock or living with an unmarried man could hurt their neighbors. Now we know the negative social effects these two living arrangements have spawned: lower marriage rates, more instability in the marriages that are enacted, more fatherless children, increased rates of domestic violence and poverty, and a vast expansion of welfare state expenses.[19]

Many believe that changing marriage by allowing gays to marry would diminish its value in the eyes of many Americans. The result could be that fewer couples would marry, leading to instability in society.

Advocates of gay marriage agree with this assessment of the dangers of illegitimacy and cohabitation. In fact, they use these statistics to support their own contention that any two people—gay or straight—who want to form a lasting relationship are better off doing so within the stable structure of a legally recognized marriage. If marriage promotes responsibility and commitment, as those who favor same-sex marriage believe, then marriage will promote responsibility and commitment for homosexuals as well.

Equal Rights and the Sanctity of Marriage

While gay-marriage proponents in states that recognize some form of legal partnership for same-sex couples see progress in these arrangements, many still view them as inferior compromises. They point to the U.S. Constitution and its promise of

equal rights to insist that nothing less than equal marriage will do. Proponents of gay marriage often equate current bans on gay marriage with bans on interracial marriage, which were not overturned by the U.S. Supreme Court until 1967. Opponents of gay marriage, however, claim that comparing gay marriage to interracial marriage employs false logic. Tony Perkins, president of the Family Research Council, quotes a Minnesota judge who ruled against a same-sex couple who used that argument to try to convince the courts that they should be allowed to marry: "In common sense and constitutional sense, there is a clear distinction between a marital restriction based merely upon race and one based upon the fundamental difference in sex."[20] Opponents of gay marriage see a great difference between a person's race, which is inborn and unchangeable, and homosexuality, which they view as a behavior. If homosexuality is a behavior, then a person is free to choose whether to engage in that behavior.

LOVE THE PERSON, NOT THE LIFESTYLE

Though often accused of hating gay people, many opponents of gay marriage explain that their actions are motivated by love rather than hate. Some vocal anti–gay marriage activists for example, acknowledge they have gay family members and maintain that their opposition to gay marriage is driven by the desire to protect homosexuals from the dangers inherent in gay relationships. Rick Bowers, pastor of a nondenominational church in Columbia, Maryland, is the head of Defend Maryland Marriage, an activist group. Bowers, too, opposes behavior, not individuals: "There are extremists who say that if a gay person were on fire you would burn in hell if you spit on them to put out the fire. But we're not like that. We love the human being. It's the lifestyle we disagree with."

Quoted in Russell Shorto, "What's Their Real Problem with Gay Marriage?" *New York Times Magazine*, June 19, 2005, p. 41.

Another argument frequently invoked by religious conservatives who oppose gay marriage is that these relationships threaten the sanctity of marriage itself. The word *sanctity* invokes strong feelings because it implies that marriage is holy or sacred, and so, by definition, blessed by God. Some people, however, counter this argument by pointing out that though members of the clergy frequently perform marriages, a religious presence is not, in fact, required to legalize a marriage. Many marriage ceremonies are performed by civil judges or clerks outside traditional religious institutions such as churches or synagogues. Moreover, proponents of gay marriage say, cultural trends clearly belie the aura of religion around many legal marriages. As Perkins explains, "It's time we were all asking just how much sanctity the law currently embodies when it allows heterosexual couples to marry strangers on reality TV shows and permits couples to be married in drive-through chapels with Elvis impersonators."[21] Besides questioning whether marriage is a religious institution, many gay-marriage advocates question the constitutionality of using religious objections to challenge gay marriage at all. The notion that matters of the church and matters of the state should not be intermingled has been fundamental to this country since its founding over two hundred years ago.

A Call for an Amendment to the Constitution

Belief in the sanctity of marriage has figured prominently in public support of an amendment to the U.S. Constitution banning gay marriage entirely. This issue was pushed to the forefront of the political arena by events that occurred in two of the most liberal states in the country: Massachusetts and California.

Encouraged by alternative weddings in other parts of the country, the mayor of Parched Flat, Utah, performs the marriage of Elmer Sturdley, his nine wives, and a goat (not pictured).

www.caglecartoons.com

© 2004 MONTE WOLVERTON

In November 2003, the Supreme Judicial Court of Massachusetts ruled in favor of seven gay couples who believed that their constitutional rights to equal treatment were being denied by the state's refusal to marry them. More than one thousand same-sex couples applied for marriage licenses in Massachusetts during the first week they were offered the following May. The uproar caused by that decision motivated President George W. Bush to renew his push for a constitutional amendment that would override the patchwork of gay-marriage legislation in individual states. Bush issued a statement after the decision in Massachusetts, saying, "Marriage is a sacred institution between a man and a woman. Today's decision of the Massachusetts Supreme Judicial Court violates this important principle. I will work with congressional leaders and others to do what is legally necessary to defend the sanctity of marriage."[22]

Bush's call for a constitutional amendment echoed the sentiments of many legislators who struggle with issues arising from the hodgepodge of legal arrangements throughout the country.

In California, Governor Gray Davis signed the state's Defense of Marriage Act in 2003, which banned gay marriage within the same two-week period that Massachusetts approved it. In an act of civil disobedience, San Francisco mayor Gavin Newsom then decided on his own that the marriage laws in California violated the equal protection rights of gays and lesbians. He authorized the city of San Francisco to issue marriage licenses to same-sex couples. Between February 12 and March 11, 2004, over four thousand same-sex couples from

An elated gay couple holds hands as they leave San Francisco City Hall in February 2004 with a marriage license.

around the state and the country obtained marriage licenses in San Francisco. However, after four weeks, the California Supreme Court voided the licenses, ruling that Newsom had overstepped his authority. The judges made it clear at the time that their decision applied only to the narrow question of Newsom's authority to make that decision and not to the larger issue of the constitutionality of state marriage laws. In March 2005, however, San Francisco Superior Court judge Richard Kramer struck down California's ban on gay marriage altogether, claiming, "It appears that no rational purpose exists for limiting marriage in this state to opposite-sex partners."[23] Gay-marriage advocates hailed Kramer's decision as a victory for equal rights.

A Constitutional Ban?

Opponents of gay marriage view both Massachusetts's legalization of gay marriage and Newsom's civil disobedience in a different light. Rather than setbacks, they view these victories as fuel that energizes the anti–gay marriage movement. Matthew Stayer, president of Liberty Council, a Florida-based group that opposes gay marriage, explains: "The Massachusetts ruling really created a backlash, and now they're on the defensive. That, combined with the issuing of gay-marriage licenses in San Francisco accelerated the pace beyond what advocates probably wanted. That has played into the hands of the pro-family movement."[24] While it would appear on the surface that legalizing gay marriage in Massachusetts would potentially be a step toward legalizing gay marriage in all fifty states, anti–gay marriage forces believe that the victory will backfire. They trust that the country as a whole is not ready to accept gay marriage and will instead be inspired to fight it at the ballot box and support a constitutional amendment to ban it permanently.

The road to a constitutional amendment, however, is long and arduous. An amendment to the Constitution requires a two-thirds majority vote in both the House and Senate followed by approval by voters in three-fourths (or thirty-eight) of the fifty states. The amendment has already been defeated once by Congress. Even many people who are uncomfortable with gay marriage stop short of supporting a constitutional ban.

A CNN poll taken shortly after Massachusetts legalized gay marriage showed that 58 percent of those polled were opposed to a constitutional amendment banning gay marriage. An editorial from the *New York Times* explains, "Even many Americans who are skittish about gay marriage do not want to enshrine intolerance as one of the nation's fundamental principles."[25] Many legal scholars point out that constitutional amendments have traditionally ensured that all citizens are treated equally under the laws of the country. This proposed constitutional amendment on the other hand, would permanently deny homosexuals one right—the right to marry the partner of one's choice—that is guaranteed to other Americans.

The possibility of a constitutional amendment banning gay marriage appears less likely the longer time goes by. Exit polls from eleven states that banned gay marriage in the November 2004 election indicated that younger voters are more likely to favor gay marriage. Gay-marriage advocates point out that those young voters will eventually become the mainstream citizens who wield the most influence on politics and social policies.

Both gay-marriage advocates and opponents are watching closely as legal cases wind their way through various courts and ballot initiatives in the fifty states. Each side has an interest in bringing this issue to the ultimate test of the U.S. Constitution. Pro–gay marriage forces believe that a constitutional test will result in a decision that equates the right to marry the partner of one's choice with the pursuit of happiness that is promised to all Americans in the Declaration of Independence. They believe that this promise will rise above religious and conservative objections to gay marriage. Those who oppose gay marriage believe just as strongly that a constitutional amendment outlawing gay marriage is inevitable. They believe that the public will recognize that marriage is by definition the legal joining of one man and one woman.

Constitution Versus States' Rights

There is a third way to view the debate about a constitutional amendment. Many believe that the solutions to the problem raised by gay marriage should not reside in the Constitution

Marriage Laws by State

Legend:

- State issues marriage licenses to same-sex couples.
- State has no explicit provision prohibiting marriages between individuals of the same sex.
- State has passed a law that defines marriage as between a man and a woman and does not honor marriages between same-sex couples from other jurisdictions.
- State has amended its state constitution to declare marriages between same-sex couples void or invalid.
- State has amended its constitution to declare marriages between same-sex couples void or invalid; has passed law defining marriage as between a man and woman; does not honor same-sex marriage.

Source: www.religioustolerance.org

Data as of 2005.

at all, but should be decided by each state individually. That way, states that are open to the idea of gay marriage could approve it, and those that are opposed could refuse to allow it. Some advocates of gay marriage believe that once voters see that allowing gay marriage does not endanger marriage in general, people will be more willing to go along with it. Even many gay-marriage proponents agree that forcing gay marriage upon states in which a majority of voters do not approve of it would doom gay marriage to failure. One thing is certain: The openness and visibility of the gay community ensures that this issue will not disappear easily from public sight.

GAY FAMILIES

While the issue of legalizing gay marriage still brews in the courts and legislatures of this country, gay families—families in which gay mothers and fathers raise children—wrestle with the legal and social issues that affect them every day. The actual number of children being raised in gay households is difficult to determine, with estimates ranging from 200,000 to over 3 million. The census of 2000 counted 594,000 same-sex households in the United States, with about one-third of the lesbian couples and over one-fifth of the male couples reportedly raising children. Most population experts agree that these numbers may represent only a small fraction of the actual number of gay families in the country, since many same-sex partners, fearing repercussions, are reluctant to reveal their true family structures.

Gay families face the same challenges that all families face as they raise their children. But, in addition, gay families grapple with some unique challenges that result from their position outside mainstream society. Society has not yet figured out exactly how to deal with gay parents who want to adopt children or the custody arrangements that result from divorces when one parent is gay. Many people question whether a child being raised in a gay household will necessarily turn out to be gay or whether children suffer damage from having a gay parent.

While various experts study the consequences of being raised in a gay household, no one disputes the fact that many gay families exist. Millions of children growing up today will be adults before all the answers are determined. In the meantime, gay families are demanding the same rights and treatment under the law as heterosexual families.

Will the Children Be Normal?

While all gay families face many of the same challenges, gay families themselves are far from homogeneous. There are many variations of the gay family: two gay fathers; two lesbian mothers; families resulting from adoption; children conceived from the egg of one parent and donor sperm; or the sperm of one parent and a surrogate mother. There are families with children from previous marriages, single parent families, and families with three or more parents when gay couples and lesbian couples who are also friends cooperate to conceive and raise each other's children. The one factor that is common to gay families, however, is that they all include at least one, if not two, gay parents.

Arguments about whether children raised in gay or lesbian households will be normal fuel the debates about whether these households should be granted the same legal protections and rights as other families. Many people fear that gay and lesbian parents do not provide healthy and safe environments for children.

A homosexual couple plays with their adopted twin daughters. Across the United States, a large number of children are being raised in gay households.

TWO MOMS, TWO DADS

Alex Morris, eleven, is one boy with four loving parents. His biological mother, Paula Morris, recently married her partner of sixteen years, Cory Pohley. His biological father, Toner Humber, lives with his partner of twenty-three years, Harvey Yaw. Alex rotates among all four parents, moving between their two houses every few days. Sometimes they all vacation together. His mother's official marriage makes Alex happy. He explains: "It is something I always wanted. I've always been around people saying, 'Oh, my parents' anniversary is this week.' It's always been the sight of two parents, married, with rings. And knowing I'd probably never experience it ever."

Quoted in Patricia Leigh Brown, "For Children of Gays, Marriage Brings Joy," *New York Times*, March 19, 2004, p. A13.

Others believe that a child who grows up in a gay household will necessarily turn out gay. An article by Susan Dominus in the *New York Times Magazine* titled "Growing Up with Mom and Mom" frames the question that is foremost in many discussions about gay families: "The children of gay parents are not just aspiring filmmakers, or dropouts, or Phi Beta Kappas [a college honor society] . . . they're also a form of evidence in the political debate. How do the children of gay parents turn out, when compared with the children of straight parents, in terms of eventual marital status, income, psychological well being?"[26] This question is central to the debate about whether communities, states, or even the country as a whole has an obligation to allow gay and lesbian families the same rights as other families.

One of the most emotionally laden debates about children raised in gay families is the question of the ultimate sexual orientation of those children: Will children of gay parents turn out to be gay themselves? Within this question lies the question of the origin of sexual orientation: Do children become gay or lesbian because they grow up in a household with a gay parent, or are some children just born gay? Since scientists have not discovered a "gay gene," no one knows for sure. But among people who are uncomfortable with homosexuality, there is a great deal of concern that a child exposed to homosexuality during his or her impressionable years will turn out to be gay. Social conservatives who would like to limit the rights of gay parents search for studies that conclude that children become gay as a result of growing up in a gay household. Gay rights activists search for studies to support their views that growing up in a gay household has no effect on a child's sexual orientation.

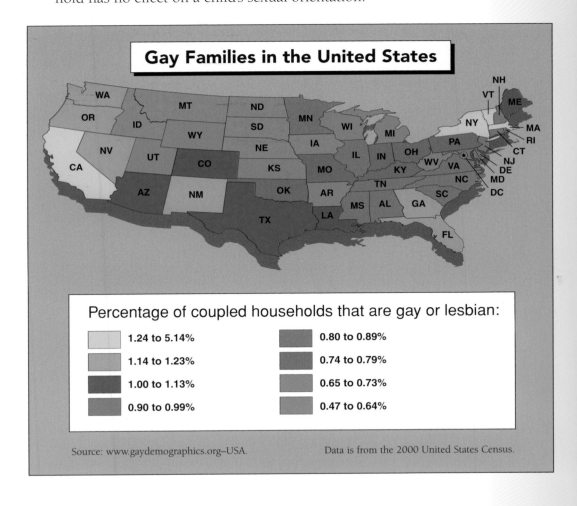

Gay Families in the United States

Percentage of coupled households that are gay or lesbian:

1.24 to 5.14%	0.80 to 0.89%
1.14 to 1.23%	0.74 to 0.79%
1.00 to 1.13%	0.65 to 0.73%
0.90 to 0.99%	0.47 to 0.64%

Source: www.gaydemographics.org–USA.   Data is from the 2000 United States Census.

The question has been studied extensively. In a book titled *The Gay Baby Boom*, authors Suzanne M. Johnson and Elizabeth O'Connor review the findings of many of the studies on the children of gay and lesbian-headed families, including the Gay and Lesbian Family Study, the largest national assessment ever performed in the country. They conclude, "There is no evidence to support the notion that having a gay or lesbian parent places a child at risk for atypical gender or sexual development in any way."[27] Their research is frequently cited by advocates for gay adoption or by gay parents fighting for custody after a divorce.

However, these results are still highly controversial and not embraced by both sides of the debate about rights for gay

A SON'S STORY

Although most gay parents try to make life as normal as possible for their children, problems can arise as children grow up. Darius Greenbacher, who was raised by lesbian parents, describes some of the challenges he faced:

My mother was always out and every school year she made sure that she told all my teachers that I came from a lesbian family. I had very few problems or issues around my upbringing until puberty set in. From about eleven until maybe thirteen, it really scared me to have lesbian parents. I felt that if people knew, they would think I was gay. And I was very, very scared and nervous about that. I grew up with a group of friends since kindergarten. We had sleep-overs at each other's houses and they knew that my mom and Judy had their own bedroom. Everyone just knew. But new friends I would make, I wasn't so open with them.

Quoted in Abigail Garner, *Families Like Mine*. New York: HarperCollins, 2004, p. 100.

families. The American College of Pediatricians, a conservative group, for example, is highly critical of studies that conclude that children are well served in gay families. In 2004 the group published a report that warns, "Children reared in homosexual households are more likely to experience sexual confusion, practice homosexual behavior, and engage in sexual experimentation."[28] They acknowledged in their conclusion, though, that while the evidence is too limited to know for sure, they believe that it would be irresponsible to lift traditional prohibitions on homosexual parenting.

Although the question about the ultimate sexual orientation of these children is still unresolved, many researchers agree that growing up in a gay household is bound to be different in some ways than growing up in a traditional family. Children from gay households often avoid telling their friends about their gay parents or face the inevitable consequences of being seen by their schoolmates as different. Benedict Carey, writing about the topic for the *New York Times*, sums up a general conclusion reached by many researchers in the field:

> One undisputed reality for children raised by gay parents is that they tend to face teasing, discrimination and bullying in the schoolyard because of who their parents are. That many of these children can navigate such nastiness, on top of the usual social and emotional squalls of growing up, and still be found as well-adjusted as their peers on standard psychological tests is remarkable in itself, some researchers say.[29]

Even if there are some definite differences between the children raised in gay and heterosexual households, many mental-health professionals contend that those differences can be positive. They point to studies that conclude that these children are more tolerant of diversity of all types and have fewer stereotypes about the roles of men and women in the home. By living with two dads, for example, a child comes to accept that typical examples of "women's work" such as washing dishes and cooking are acceptable tasks for men.

An adopted teen sings hymns alongside her gay parents during a Unitarian church service. Teens in gay households have been the subjects of numerous research studies.

But just as gay rights advocates underline the positive differences, conservatives highlight the negative effects of growing up in a gay household. They believe that as these children enter their teen years, they are more prone to depression, anxiety, and substance abuse than are teens raised in heterosexual households. Clearly, these studies all depend on information that can be interpreted in various ways. Often both sides of the debate about whether gay families should have the same rights as other families use the same evidence to support their own agendas.

Since support for the rights of gay families often hinges on the knowledge about whether the children benefit or suffer harm from these still-controversial partnerships, the outcome of these debates is watched with keen interest on all sides. Some people object to the debate entirely. Many families, children, and even experts in the field wonder whether it is fair to study these children and how they turn out before making decisions about granting gay families rights that are automatic for other families. Lisa Bennet, deputy director for Human Rights

Campaign's FamilyNet, thinks it is not. She argues, "The issues of equal rights should rest on principle, not on research. There is no other population that you can look at and say they have certain rights because the children turned out in X or Y way."[30] Yet, at the same time, every side of the debate about equal rights for gay families continues to scour the research to support its position. Decisions affecting the lives of millions of children, both born and unborn, await the answers to these questions.

Gay Adoption

While researchers seek to determine the long-term impact on children growing up in gay households, lawmakers continue to address the many legal issues that arise daily related to gay families. Since adoption is one of the most common arrangements for gay families, issues surrounding it attract a great deal of attention from both lawmakers and the public.

A lesbian couple smiles as their three adopted children come down a slide. Supporters and opponents of gay adoption both maintain they have the best interests of children at heart.

In 1999, forty-six thousand children from national public child welfare agencies were placed in permanent adoptive homes. No one knows exactly how many of those homes included gay parents since in the search for willing homes, social workers often overlook or do not ask for that information. Furthermore, statistics on gay adoption are hard to gather, since the route to adoption takes many paths. Besides public agencies, families travel overseas to adopt children, adopt through private agencies, or even adopt through personal arrangements overseen by lawyers and finalized in courts.

Both sides of the adoption debate insist that their primary focus is the best interest of the children. They agree that children fare best when raised in loving, supportive homes. But opinions vary widely on just what constitutes an appropriate home in which to raise a child. Social service workers in public agencies in many states follow the guidelines of the Child Welfare League of America, which read: "Applicants should be assessed on the basis of their abilities to successfully parent a child needing family membership and not on their race, ethnicity or culture, income, age, marital status, religion, appearance, differing lifestyles, or sexual orientation."[31] Policies in some states are unwritten, leaving it to social workers and judges to determine just which families are suitable for raising adopted children.

THE BASIC BUILDING BLOCK

"The traditional family—one father, one mother, and their natural or adopted children—is the basic building block of society. Not just our society, but society as a whole."

Citizens for Community Values, "The Homosexual Issue: Where Do We Stand? And Why?" www.ccv.org/Homosexuality Where_ CCV_Stands.htm.

Only one state, Florida, explicitly forbids gay adoption. Steven Lofton and his partner Roger Croteau challenged Florida's 1977 law banning gay adoption when they appealed to the U.S. Supreme Court to overturn the ban. Lofton and Croteau hoped to adopt a thirteen-year-old boy they had raised since infancy. Lofton, a pediatric nurse, is licensed in Florida to take in foster children and has been named outstanding foster parent of the year by the agency that placed the boy in his home. In January 2005, the U.S. Supreme Court refused to hear the challenge, effectively dashing Lofton's and Croteau's chances of adopting the boy. Florida still permits gays and lesbians to serve as foster parents, but children in foster care, including this particular child, face the uncertainty of possible adoption by another family.

Wide-Ranging Debate

Conservative groups approve of Florida's legal stance on gay adoption. Ed Vitagliano, a spokesman for the American Family Association in Tupelo, Mississippi, argues that a two-parent household consisting of a mother and a father is in the best interests of any child. He explains, "We think it is best for a child to have a male and a female as parents. A man and a woman each bring something unique to the parenting role, and that is really what children should have by design of God."[32] Other conservative groups such as the Family Research Council agree. They point out that children who have been in the public welfare system have special emotional and psychological needs that are best met in traditional families.

While Florida is the only state that bans gays and lesbians outright from adopting children, laws vary widely in other states. New Hampshire, Mississippi, and Utah permit single gays and lesbians to adopt but explicitly forbid gay couples to adopt jointly. New Jersey adoption law, on the other hand, forbids sexual orientation and marital status from being used to discriminate against potential adoptive parents. New Jersey, New York, and California allow second-parent adoption, which gives gay and lesbians the opportunity to legally adopt the children who have been adopted previously by their same-sex partners.

Proponents of gay adoption agree that the well-being of children who have been in the public system is paramount, but argue that gays and lesbians are excellent resources for children who have had difficult childhood experiences. According to Joan Heifetz Hollinger, a leading scholar on adoption law and practice, gay families provide a unique perspective: "Often, people who themselves have had a difficult time being accepted or have faced criticism have special insight or empathy.

Rather than excluding, one might consider that some people, because of their sexual orientation, may be better able to serve these children."[33] One undisputed fact is that many gay families adopt children who are older, biracial, or have disabilities or other health problems. Gay men and women are often so interested in becoming parents that they are ready and willing to adopt these children who are passed over by traditional would-be parents.

Concerns about gay adoption persist, however. Many people are worried about gay and lesbian couples raising children whose gender differs from their own, feeling uncomfortable about gay men raising young girls or lesbians raising sons. The Oregon Defense of Marriage Coalition answered questions about this issue on its Web site. In response to a question about whether children are better off having loving parents regardless of their sexual orientation, the answer is unequivocally negative:

> The most loving mother in the world cannot teach a little boy how to be a man. Likewise, the most loving man cannot teach a little girl how to be a woman. A gay man cannot teach his son how to love and care for a woman. A lesbian cannot teach her daughter how to love a man or know what to look for in a good husband. Is love enough to help two gay dads guide their daughter through her first menstrual cycle? Like a mom, they cannot comfort her by sharing their first experience. Little boys and girls need the loving daily influence of both male and female parents to become who they are meant to be.[34]

Unsupported Claims

Research, however does not support these claims, which are pervasive among conservative groups opposed to gay and lesbian adoption. Many studies have compared the sexual identity of children raised in gay and lesbian and heterosexual families. These studies consistently demonstrate that children who grow up in gay and lesbian households identify themselves correctly

as boys or girls, have friends, and play in ways that are typical for their biological sex. In fact, many gay couples take great care to ensure that their little girls have frequent contact with sisters, aunts, and female friends. Likewise, lesbians raising sons make sure that their boys grow up spending time with male role models.

Some gay and lesbian parents avoid issues relating to adoption through alternative arrangements. Many homosexuals who crave a biological connection to their offspring resort to a surrogate or sperm donor. For example, two men might hire a female surrogate to have either her egg or a donor egg fertilized with one or a mixture of both of their sperm; she then carries the baby to term. The infant is then adopted by one or both of the gay men. Similarly, a lesbian couple may decide that one of them will use donor sperm to fertilize one of their own eggs and then give birth to the resulting child. However, both of these options are expensive if facilitated by an agency such as Growing Generations, the first surrogacy agency founded specifically for gay men in 1996.

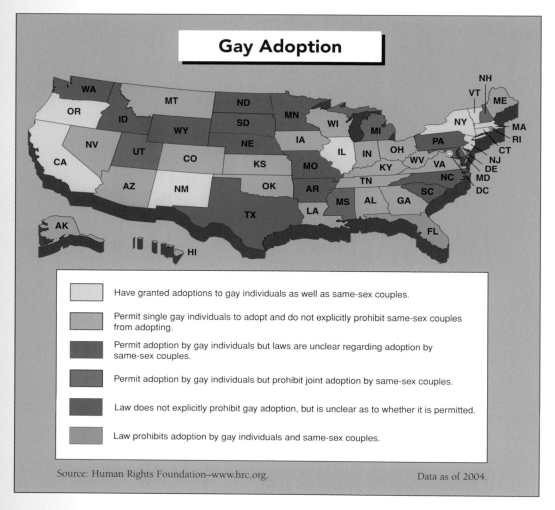

Gay Adoption

Legend:
- Have granted adoptions to gay individuals as well as same-sex couples.
- Permit single gay individuals to adopt and do not explicitly prohibit same-sex couples from adopting.
- Permit adoption by gay individuals but laws are unclear regarding adoption by same-sex couples.
- Permit adoption by gay individuals but prohibit joint adoption by same-sex couples.
- Law does not explicitly prohibit gay adoption, but is unclear as to whether it is permitted.
- Law prohibits adoption by gay individuals and same-sex couples.

Source: Human Rights Foundation–www.hrc.org.   Data as of 2004.

Hiring a female surrogate through the agency costs between $50,000 and $70,000. Since its founding, Growing Generations has assisted in about three hundred births nationwide. This option is also expensive for lesbians who go through an agency in search of a sperm donor. Many gays and lesbians bypass the agency altogether and find homosexual friends of the opposite sex who are willing to parent their children. Children who result from these arrangements between their gay and lesbian parents refer to themselves as "bothies," since both of their parents are homosexual.

Who Gets Custody of the Children?

These arrangements are relatively rare, however. The overwhelming majority of the 2 million gay parents are raising children from earlier heterosexual marriages. For this reason, there is an urgent need to establish legal guidelines for child custody decisions after a divorce. In the 1970s and 1980s, a gay man or lesbian was considered an unfit parent and usually denied custody. Those rigid policies have become more flexible in the last twenty years or so as they have begun to reflect an increased tolerance and recognition of gay families. Rather than strictly forbidding a gay parent access to his or her child, courts increasingly consider the best interest of the child to guide custody decisions.

The difficulty is determining what that best interest is. Some judges believe that a child is best served by maintaining a relationship with both natural parents whenever possible. In other jurisdictions, court decisions reflect the belief that a child's best interest is not served by spending time with a gay parent. Many gay and lesbian parents have had their custody limited entirely or restricted to supervised visits with their children. Theron McGriff, for example, a father in Idaho, took his custody case to the Idaho Supreme Court in 2002. He was appealing the decision of a county judge that awarded his ex-wife full custody of their two school-age daughters as long as he lived with his gay partner. Two years later, the court upheld the decision. Although McGriff lost his custody battle, gay activists were pleased that the court's ruling made it clear that sexual orientation alone cannot be used to determine custody decisions. Many other states have similar policies.

No Problem

"I had two moms who loved me, and because my friends thought it was fine, and my parents thought it was fine, then I thought it was fine. It wasn't a problem."

Peter Hams, 24, quoted in Jack Thomas, "Not Better, Not Worse, Just Different," *San Diego Union-Tribune*, June 13, 2004, p. E1.

In this 2005 photo, a lesbian identified in court papers as K.M. (right) hugs her attorney. The California Supreme Court had just ruled that K.M. and her ex-partner were both to be legal parents of their children. Lower courts had granted legal parenthood only to the ex-partner.

Another situation in which custody can be complicated is when gay families split up after either adopting children or giving birth to children by donor insemination or surrogacy. A case in San Francisco illustrates clearly how the legal system has not yet caught up to the reality of gay parenting. The case revolved around two women who decided to implant the eggs from one into the uterus of the other after fertilizing them with donor sperm. This arrangement was intended to give both women a biological role in their children's births. The woman who carried the eggs to term gave birth to twin girls. When the relationship ended, the birth mother was granted full custody of the eight-year-old girls, because the genetic mother had never legally adopted them. The *San Diego Union-Tribune* reports on the case: "Shannon Mintner, an attorney for the National Center for Lesbian Rights, said if the losing mother were a man, she would have been awarded rights to the children who have moved with the birth mother to Massachusetts and have little contact with the other woman."[35] In California, the domestic partnership law that went into effect in January 2005 will help resolve such child custody disputes, since registered domestic partners will have access to family courts for establishing custody arrangements. However, many states are still searching for ways to deal with the issue of child custody for same-sex couples who split up.

Legal Conflicts

As gay families become increasingly common, the legal system— local courts, state legislatures, and the federal government— confronts issues that pit strong and conflicting opinions against each other. Many people believe that all families, whether formed by gays and lesbians, single parents, or traditional parents consisting of a mother, a father, and their biological children, deserve the same rights and access to the legal system. Others believe firmly that growing up in a gay household goes against the best interests of children, and, therefore, society has no moral or legal obligation to approve gay adoption or grant custody of children to gay parents. Until the bigger questions about the origin of homosexuality are resolved, the conflicts about the legal rights of gay families in America are bound to continue.

GAY RIGHTS IN SCHOOLS

Children from all families, except those who are educated at home, attend the nation's schools. Many families that include either a gay parent or a gay child argue that their children are denied an education equivalent to that of children from heterosexual families because they face harassment, isolation, and discrimination. Solutions range from specific antidiscrimination policies to school programs that educate others and teach tolerance. Some gay rights advocates even support taking the highly controversial step of creating special schools for gay teens. Others dismiss these measures, claiming that children from gay families face problems no worse than those faced by all children in school. They believe that existing antidiscrimination policies are sufficient to protect all students, including those who are gay or whose families include gay members. While these issues are debated both locally and nationally, students go to school each day, learning both academics and the skills of navigating a culture that includes people of many religions, races, traditions, and ideas.

The issue of how to deal with gay youth in schools has become part of the public consciousness only in the last twenty years or so. Before the 1970s, few students identified themselves as homosexual because the gay and lesbian community was still hidden from view. As gay and lesbian adults began claiming their rights to be protected from discrimination and to be treated as equals to other citizens, however, gay youth also became more vocal and more visible. But the presence of gay and lesbian students was not ordinarily welcomed. Gay students have always faced the reality that they might be rejected by their fellow students, shamed by their teachers and administrators, and threatened by a culture that does not accept them.

This culture of discrimination toward gay youth has had serious effects. A study titled *Hatred in the Hallways*, published in 2001 by Human Rights Watch, details the fear and humiliation suffered by gay and lesbian youth in schools. The introduction to the report explains the damage that the constant fear and harassment can wreak on students who are still struggling with issues of self-identity typical for their age. According to the report, "Gay youth spend an inordinate amount of energy plotting how to get safely to and from school, how to avoid the hallways when other students are present so they can avoid slurs and shoves, how to cut gym class to escape being beaten up—in short, how to become invisible so they will not be verbally and physically attacked."[36]

Thousands of gay high school students in Boston take part in the 2000 youth pride march, demanding respect and equal rights.

Several studies of gay and lesbian youth have found that as a result of this ongoing fear of abuse, gay and lesbian students face a significantly higher risk than do their heterosexual peers for suicide, alcohol and drug abuse, running away from home, and dropping out of school. The report concluded that the public schools have failed to protect these students effectively.

The Challenge of Protecting Gay Students

The reasons that many schools have been slow to take steps to address the problems of discrimination against gay students are complex. Some school officials blame the very students who are being abused. They feel that these students behave in ways that purposefully bring attention to themselves and reason that if they do not like the consequences, they should change their behavior. Also, demanding that school officials take action against students who are harassing their gay and lesbian peers often means forcing them to confront their own prejudices and intervene in situations they do not personally find objectionable.

Another reason schools are sometimes reluctant to broach the subject of the rights of gay students is that they risk offending other parents who do not want their children exposed to the topic of homosexuality, even for the purpose of teaching tolerance. There is simply no way to educate students about treating their gay and lesbian peers respectfully without discussing homosexuality. Many parents object to raising this topic in school at all, since they believe that gay rights affects such a small proportion of the overall school population. They believe that their own moral values, many based on religious teachings, are ignored when their children are forced to participate in discussions about homo-sexuality or are condemned for their opinions that homosexuality is unacceptable. At the opposite end of

THE EXTRA MAN

"When I knew I would be holding up my drawing to the entire class, I drew my mom and dad, but not my dad's partner. I was not ready to explain why my family picture had an extra man in it."

Abigail Garner, *Families Like Mine*. New York: HarperCollins, 2004, p. 97.

HOMOPHOBIA IN HIGH SCHOOL

A report by the international watchdog organization Human Rights Watch details the many ways that gay and lesbian students can suffer at school because of their sexual orientation. The account of Alix M. is typical:

> Beginning in middle school, I became really depressed. At first I didn't know why. Didn't have a clue. But I knew it wasn't okay to be gay. No one was out at my middle school, but I heard lots of slurs all the time. Lots of homophobic comments. I was scared. Scared to be a lesbian. Scared to be out at school. Scared of being so alone. My grades started to fall. A counselor talked to me about my grades. I had always been a good student. But she didn't give me any opening to talk about sexuality. I needed to get information.
>
> Now I am a senior in high school. It's better now for me. But public spaces are the worst. I hear things all the time. The halls have a very male macho feeling—very sexist. I also had one teacher who would say "that's so gay" instead of saying "that's so stupid."

Human Rights Watch, *Hatred in the Hallways*, 2001. http:/hrw.org/reports/2001/uslgbt.

the spectrum are parents and educators who believe that children begin to form at a very young age the social attitudes that they will carry with them for the rest of their lives. For that reason, they believe that it is important to begin educating even the youngest students about the importance of tolerance for all lifestyles.

This conflict was played out when the state of New York was considering the passage of its Dignity for All Students Act in 2002. The bill, which began in the state assembly, proposed educating all students in kindergarten through grade twelve about bias and discrimination on the basis of race, religion, ethnic background, sexual orientation, and disability. Many opponents claimed that this bill was merely a gay rights bill thinly disguised as an attempt to protect students from any type of discrimination.

A church group condemns homosexuality outside a Las Vegas high school during the staging of a school play involving homosexual themes.

The National Non-Sectarian Council of Pro-Family Activists, a conservative group that opposes homosexuality education in schools, explains its viewpoint in a press release: "The bill, if enacted, would place into New York schools state-issued teaching materials (including textbooks) that would present such things as homosexuality as normal, acceptable behavior. It would also label those who disagree with this opinion as bigoted and intolerant."[37] The bill was ultimately defeated.

This conflict between protecting gay and lesbian students and the rights of students who object to the discussion entirely is difficult to reconcile. It pits the strong emotions of gay rights advocates against the equally strong opinions of those whose belief in the traditional family overrides objections to antigay discrimination. In addition, since the argument centers on the rights of students who are younger than eighteen, the opinions of their parents hold great weight.

The American Civil Liberties Union Takes on Gay Rights at School

The American Civil Liberties Union (ACLU), founded in the 1920s, has assumed a major role in providing legal support to gay and lesbian youth in their ongoing struggle to gain protection in hostile school environments. The ACLU's mission is to preserve and protect the constitutional rights of American citizens. Though decisions about what to teach in the schools are dictated by individual states and their school districts, rights of individual citizens in this country are specified in the Bill of Rights, the first ten amendments to the Constitution. These rights include the freedom of speech and expression and the right to form social and political organizations.

The ACLU represented five students in northern California in 2003 when they sued their high school in Santa Clara County for refusing to take action to protect them from ongoing antigay harassment. According to an ACLU press release, "The students, four girls and one boy were repeatedly abused both physically and verbally. One student was hospitalized after a group of male students shouted insults and hit and kicked him in front of nearby school employees."[38] The decision by the U.S. Court of Appeals for the Ninth Circuit stated that teachers and administrators must take steps to eliminate harassment when they learn that lesbian and gay students are abused at school. This action was historic because it was unprecedented. It was the first time that schools were specifically held accountable by the federal government for the way gay and lesbian students are treated while they are on school grounds.

A HOSTILE ENVIRONMENT

"Militant teachers and pupils are creating a hostile environment for students who hold faith-based or traditional values that view homosexuality as immoral."

Brad Dacus, president, Pacific Justice Institute, quoted in Pacific Justice Institute, "High School Teachers Promote Homosexuality to Captive Audience." www.pji.org/resources/news/focus-details.cfm?ID=PR050202a.

Utah's ACLU chapter was involved in 2004 in a case involving Jason Atwood, a senior at Copper Hills High School in West Jordan, who was determined to attend school dances with a same-sex date even though his school's administration put obstacles in his path. The vice principal at the school told Atwood that he would need a note from his parents acknowledging their awareness that his choice of date might present security problems. He was also told that he and his date would both need parental approval every time they attended a school dance. The Web site Tolerance.org details the reaction of Utah's ACLU: "Dani Eyer, executive director of Utah's ACLU chapter said such bias and resistance come from school administrators more often than students. And many times, administrators justify their actions by claiming discriminatory policies are designed to protect gay students from harassment."[39] In this case, pressure from the ACLU, along with a student protest that was covered by newspapers and television, exerted enough pressure on the principal that

A mother wipes away her tears as she listens to her daughter share with a congressional committee the problems she has faced as a lesbian high school student.

he reversed his policy. Atwood attended both the Valentine's Day dance and his senior prom with a same-sex date.

There are others, however, who believe that the ACLU does not defend the constitutional rights of everyone. In Boyd County, Kentucky, the Alliance Defense Fund (ADF) sued the school district in April 2005 for an ACLU-supported plan to require all high school and middle school students to attend mandatory gay tolerance classes. The ADF lawsuit claimed that the ACLU agreement violated the free speech of parents and students who wished to speak out against homosexuality. It also maintained that parental rights were violated by requiring attendance at the training, which involved a video featuring Boyd County school employees explaining that homosexuality is an inborn, unchangeable trait. Tim York, president of Defenders Voice, a local traditional values organization, explains why his organization opposed the training: "About 20 percent of it was pure homosexual agenda. Organizations like the ACLU should not be allowed to tell parents what their children must learn. Where are the parental rights in this whole thing?"[40]

Uniting Gay Students Across the Country

While individual schools and districts struggle with the conflicts between the rights of gay and lesbian students and those who find homosexuality objectionable, one organization has become increasingly powerful in schools across the country. The Gay, Lesbian, and Straight Education Network (GLSEN) has grown from a small group to one encompassing hundreds of thousands of students, educators, policy makers, and others across the nation. Its mission is to create safe schools for all gay and lesbian students. Since it became a national organization in 1990, it has had a major impact on school policy and has expanded to link more than seven hundred student-run clubs across the nation. In 1997 GLSEN director Kevin Jennings met with President Bill Clinton for a private meeting in which the issue of antigay bias in the schools was raised for the first time at the White House. The GLSEN also lobbied state legislators in California to pass the Student Protection Act, which legally required schools to protect lesbian and gay students from discrimination and harassment.

In 2004 the GLSEN issued its first *State of the States* report, which analyzed state policies and ranked the states according to how well they protected their gay and lesbian student populations. Only eight states and the District of Columbia were found to have statewide laws in place that afforded legal protection to students based on sexual orientation. Although the report found that a growing number of states were making efforts to curtail harassment and discrimination, forty-two states received failing grades. A year earlier, the GLSEN National School Climate Survey found that gay and lesbian students were 40 percent more likely than heterosexual students to skip school because of fear for their personal safety.

Groups such as GLSEN are not embraced universally. In fact, conservative groups such as Citizens for Community Values (CCV) sometimes blame them for using the schools as a platform to normalize homosexual behavior. In a statement on its Web site, CCV pointed out that characterizing disapproval of homosexuality as biased or discriminatory silences students who believe that homosexuality is wrong. According to CCV,

> On a regular basis in public schools, under the guise of anti-bias or multi-cultural education, simple statements expressing disapproval of homosexuality for moral, religious or health reasons are categorized as 'hate,' 'homophobia,' or 'discrimination.' . . . The reason that the homosexual activists' agenda concentrates so heavily on schools is obvious. In the workplace and political arenas, some opposition to normalization of homosexual behavior still exists. With a well-executed agenda in our schools, that opposition will be non-existent in the next generation.[41]

CCV views the actions of GLSEN and other groups as purposeful attacks on traditional family values to undermine the moral and religious foundations of society.

A Special School for Lesbian and Gay Students

In a radical departure from in-school programs promoted by GLSEN and other similarly minded organizations, one public

In 2003 the executive director of the ACLU of Kentucky (far right) discusses the filing of a lawsuit to force the state school board to permit homosexual clubs to operate on school property.

school in New York City was created specifically for gay and lesbian students. Harvey Milk High School, financed by the Hetrick-Martin Institute, a social service agency in New York, opened its doors in 1984 with two small classrooms and fifty gay and lesbian students. At first the school did not even grant high school diplomas. It employed one instructor who helped gay runaways earn their high school equivalency degrees. Then, in 2001, Mayor Rudolph Giuliani began the process of expanding the school into an accredited four-year high school. Two years and $3.2 million later, the expansion transformed HMHS into a full-fledged public high school with one hundred students. Giuliani's successor, New York mayor Michael Bloomberg, approves of the high school's expansion: "I think everybody feels that it's a good idea because some of the kids who are gays and lesbians have been constantly harassed and beaten in other schools. It lets them get an education without having to worry."[42] Celebrities such as Senator Hillary Rodham Clinton and actress Susan Sarandon joined Bloomberg in enthusiastic support of the high school's expansion and mission to educate the city's gay and lesbian students.

But not everyone shared Bloomberg's enthusiasm for the exclusive school. Criticism, in fact, came from many quarters, including gay rights activists, conservative Democrats, and Republicans. One strong advocate of both gay rights and public education, Jonathan Turley, a professor of constitutional law at George Washington University, was one of Harvey Milk's most vocal critics. He criticized the concept of exiling gay students from the public school system and compared it to the "separate but equal" era in the schools. He

MODERN-DAY SEGREGATION

Some observers hailed the establishment of gays-only Harvey Milk High School in New York City as a positive step toward creating a safe learning environment for homosexual students. Others, however, including legal scholar Jonathan Turley, say that such a school undermines the goal of accepting and assimilating gays in society:

> For those of us who have supported gay rights, the announcement of the new high school is baffling. There is no question that gay students are often the targets of harassment and even violence. But a segregated school is the worst possible way of addressing the problem. The creation of the school seems to be an acknowledgment that the city cannot perform its mandatory responsibility to supply a safe and healthy environment for all students. The city's chosen solution is not to correct those failings but to remove the students, as if they are the source of the problem. Ironically, the recent legal gains of the gay rights movement are due largely to the assimilation of gays into American culture and society. This process of assimilation is probably most important on the high school level for both straight and gay students. This is the last controlled environment for teenagers before they enter the workforce or college. It is also when the most lasting values and impressions are created. High schools are meant to educate students not just in academic subjects but citizenship.

Jonathan Turley, "A High School for Gays Reeks of Segregation."
www.jonathanturley.com/Articles/Gay_high_school_reeks_of_segregation.htm.

In 2003 hundreds of people stage a rally to support students on the first day of class at New York's Harvey Milk High School, the country's first public all-gay high school.

argued that segregating gay students from their heterosexual peers was just as bad as enrolling black students and white students in separate schools even if the intention was positive. Turley blames Bloomberg for taking the easy way out: "I think Harvey Milk High School is an enormous cop-out by the Bloomberg administration. It would be far more expensive to deal with the underlying problem: to train teachers, to monitor classrooms, to punish prejudicial students. All of that comes with high financial and political costs; it is much easier to isolate these students and claim it as a benefit."[43] Turley was joined by many others who criticized the creation of a school for a group of students who face discrimination. In an interview with the *New York Post*, Michael Long, chairman of the Conservative Party of New York State, expressed his own criticism by questioning whether there are special teaching methods aimed at gay and lesbian students.

In addition to conflicts arising from the segregation of students, more controversy was generated by the $3.2 million expense for the school's expansion at a time when the city was suffering financial woes. In August 2003, Democratic state senator Ruben Diaz Sr., a Pentecostal minister from the Bronx, north of Manhattan, sued the city over the high school. Diaz, who also headed the New York Hispanic Clergy Association, felt that it was unfair of the city to devote millions of dollars to a high school that serviced just one hundred students when so many other schools were in dire need of funds. Diaz explains, "Teachers take money from their own pockets to buy equipment because they don't provide the teachers with the equipment—no books, no pencils, there's nothing for the students. You are leaving some kids behind."[44] He pointed out that Harvey Milk, on the other hand, had

HIDING THE TRUTH

Students watch their teachers closely and take cues from them, many of which are quite subtle. They learn both information and attitudes: attitudes toward learning and attitudes toward other students. If a teacher does not like one of their classmates, the chances are high, especially in the earlier grades, that the other students in the class will not treat that student very well. Korri, a fifteen-year-old student, explains why she feels she has to hide the fact that her mother is gay:

> I think maybe five percent of my school, tops, is not homophobic. But I am not brave enough to tell them about my mom or to even ridicule them for making gay jokes. "Gay" is pretty much an insult word at my school and even teachers are not afraid to show their homophobic side. I had one teacher once tell me that gay people *want* to be normal but cannot be. I wanted to shout, "They are normal," but I was too chicken. Everybody in the class pretty much agreed with her, which made me mad.

Quoted in Abigail Garner, *Families Like Mine*. New York: HarperCollins, 2004, p. 112.

enough money to pay for new high-tech equipment, air conditioning, and the best teachers. Diaz's arguments, however, were countered by others who accused him of homophobia. They pointed to his history of opposition to gay causes, including his disapproval of the celebration of the twenty-fifth anniversary of the Stonewall rebellion. He argued at the time that the festivities would help spread diseases such as AIDS among the celebrants. Opponents also used Diaz's support for a constitutional amendment banning gay marriage as further evidence of his antigay bias.

The Harvey Milk High School case is still before the New York State Supreme Court. But although the case has not yet been decided, the lawsuit has resulted in changes to the information dispensed by the school to prospective students. Students are no longer recruited based on their sexual orientation, and the school Web site has stopped referring to the school as a haven for gay students. However, despite these changes, only one student enrolled at Harvey Milk High School in 2005 claimed to be heterosexual.

A Tale of Two T-shirts

The struggle for gay rights in schools can be painted in broad strokes, such as the creation of an entire school for gay students, or in small details, such as an item of clothing that someone pulls out of the drawer to wear to school. Small personal choices sometimes create conflicts when they blur the boundaries between one student's right to free speech and free expression and another's right to be protected from discrimination. This collision between one person's right to be protected and another's right to free expression is being played out over a small item of clothing—the T-shirt—that many students wear to school almost every day.

In one case, a sixteen-year-old student in Missouri was disciplined for wearing a pro-gay T-shirt to school that featured a pink triangle—a symbol for gay rights—and the words "Make a Difference." He was told to turn the shirt inside out to obscure the message or to go home and change. Instead, he traded shirts with a friend. When he came to school the following week with a different gay pride shirt, he was ordered not to return to school wearing clothing that supports gay rights.

The ACLU of Kansas and Western Missouri filed a lawsuit on his behalf against his high school, claiming that the school had violated the student's constitutional right to free expression. According to the *New York Times*, the student issued a statement through the ACLU which says, in part, "The school has let other students wear anti-gay T-shirts, and I understand that they have a right to do that. I just want the same right. I think tolerating each others' differences is a key part in teaching students how to become good citizens."[45] That case, which pits the student's First Amendment right to free expression against the school's authority, has not yet been decided.

In a twist on the Missouri case, Tyler Chase Harper, a student at Poway High School in Southern California, has also filed a lawsuit in federal court concerning his right to wear a T-shirt, this shirt bearing an antigay message. Harper wore the shirt with the message "Homosexuality is shameful. Romans 1:27. Be ashamed" the day after other students at Poway High had participated in a national observance to promote tolerance toward gays and lesbians. Harper's lawyer, Robert Tyler, explained that Harper wore the T-shirt because he cares about his fellow students, not because he bore them ill will. Tyler said, "He comes not with a heart of hate, but with a heart of compassion."[46] The school district's lawyer argued that Harper's compassion for his fellow students could have been expressed in a more positive way, and that schools have a state mandate to teach tolerance and prevent harassment. That case is also still moving through the courts.

Complex Issues

Issues of student rights in schools are complicated by the fact that most students are still minors. During the school day, schools are responsible for the safety and well-being of students, as well as their academic learning. This responsibility requires adults who are in positions of authority to tread a delicate line that allows all students to feel that they have a voice and that they are respected, even if their opinions are unpopular. The boundaries between free speech and harassment, or free expression and discrimination, need to be reexamined constantly as the opinions of students from various backgrounds are expressed. It is a complex task.

CHAPTER 5

GAY RIGHTS IN THE WORKPLACE

Gay and lesbian children eventually graduate from school, get jobs, and work to support their families. However, despite many gains in civil rights in the last few decades, gays and lesbians continue to experience discrimination in the workplace. They are passed over for promotions, fired, harassed, and insulted because of their sexual orientation. Although no federal law specifically prohibits discrimination in the workplace due to sexual orientation, fourteen states do offer protection to lesbian and gay workers. Moreover, national polls consistently report that more than three-fourths of voters support equal rights in the workplace for gay and lesbian Americans.

Despite the lack of state and federal protections from workplace discrimination, many large companies have taken steps on their own to eliminate discrimination. Some companies offer health benefits to workers' same-sex partners. Others have written elaborate internal policies designed to promote diversity among company employees. While gay rights activists believe these steps represent progress, those who object to homosexuality feel that their own rights are violated when they are forced to silence their opposition to these policies. This backlash among conservative employees has become more evident in recent years. Both large and small businesses tread a delicate line to satisfy all their employees, investors, and customers without risking the loss of skilled workers and loyal customers.

Federal Workplace Rights for Gays and Lesbians

Although the census of 2000 made it clear that gay and lesbian Americans live in every state in the country, as it now stands, there are no federal laws in place protecting workers

A woman visits a booth at a convention of large corporations that openly support homosexual rights.

from discrimination due to sexual orientation. In 1964 Congress passed the Civil Rights Act, which made it illegal to discriminate on the basis of race or religion. At that time, sexual orientation was not specifically included as a category in need of protection.

Several civil rights groups are pressuring Congress now to repair that omission by passing the Employment Non-Discrimination Act (ENDA). ENDA would ensure that gay and lesbian workers receive equal treatment in the workplace that would protect them from antigay job discrimination. The Human Rights Campaign, an organization that supports the rights of gays and lesbians, has been joined by many other powerful voices to lobby Congress to pass this legislation. Coretta Scott King, wife of the slain civil rights leader Martin Luther King Jr., was one of those voices. Before her death in 2006, she said, "I support the Employment Non-Discrimination Act because I believe that freedom and justice cannot be parceled out in pieces to suit political convenience. As my husband, Martin Luther King Jr. said, 'injustice anywhere is a threat to justice everywhere.' Like Martin, I don't believe you can stand for freedom for one group of people and deny it to others."[47]

King's support was important, but not unique. During the 107th Congress, the Committee on Health, Education, Labor, and Pensions, which has both Democratic and Republican members, recommended that the entire Senate consider ENDA for passage. A recommendation for a bill's passage from a Senate committee is considered crucial to its ultimate success.

ENDA also has the support of the Leadership Conference on Civil Rights (LCCR), many religious organizations, women's groups, and labor unions. Other bills before Congress that will benefit gays and lesbians in the workplace include the Domestic Partnership Benefits and Obligations Act and the Domestic Partner Health Plan Beneficiaries Act, both of which would guarantee that same-sex partners receive health and other benefits equivalent to those of their heterosexual coworkers.

While supporters of gay rights in the workplace closely watch these bills, the federal government itself has a spotty record of offering workplace protections to its gay employees, both civil and military. For example, a gay postal worker in Detroit was harassed and beaten at work because of his sexual orientation. When he took his employer to court to collect damages, he was told that while he had clearly suffered discrimination, homosexuality was not included in a category of discrimination that was prohibited. He lost his case.

Don't Ask, Don't Tell

Congress approved one of the federal government's most controversial policies regarding gay rights in 1993 during the administration of President Bill Clinton. Known as Don't Ask, Don't Tell, the policy prohibits the military from asking outright about the sexual orientation of any service person. The military is, however, permitted to discharge a service person that is openly gay or admits that he or she is homosexual. Clinton and many liberal Democrats argued at the time the legislation was approved that a person's sexual orientation had no bearing on his or her ability to serve the country or prepare for battle. Those who disagreed countered that the strength of the military depended heavily on the mutual trust and confidence among soldiers. Those who opposed allowing gay soldiers in the service believed that the mutual confidence and trust would be diminished if heterosexual soldiers were forced to share showers and bunks with open homosexuals. Don't Ask, Don't Tell was considered a compromise between legislators who were in favor of allowing gays to serve openly in the military and those who were reluctant to change the long-standing antigay bias in the country's armed forces.

Since the policy was adopted, more than ten thousand service members have been discharged, according to the Servicemembers Legal Defense Network (SLDN), a gay rights group that monitors the armed forces. However, leaders on both sides of the debate agree that the number of discharges for same-sex orientation or behavior has declined dramatically since the September 11, 2001, terrorist attacks on the United States. Kathi Wescott, senior counsel for law and policy at the SLDN, points to the decline as evidence that the policy is enforced inconsistently: "These numbers clearly show that military commanders value good service members during a time of war, whether the service members are gay or straight."[48] Wescott's group claims that the rate of discharges since September 11 has dropped more than 45 percent.

An Expensive Loss

Others who oppose discharging troops because of their sexual orientation cite the manpower shortage resulting from conflicts overseas as further reason to question the wisdom of discharging troops because they reveal they are homosexual. Representative Martin T. Meehan, the ranking Democrat on a House Armed Services subcommittee on terrorism, has raised his voice against this policy, which targets gays and lesbians during a period of global political uncertainty. He said that the armed forces could not "afford to lose qualified service members for reasons that have nothing to do with their ability or willingness to serve our country. At a time when our military is facing a critical manpower shortage, it is outrageous that our national security policy remains driven by discrimination and not military necessity."[49]

Replacing highly trained and skilled service members is expensive. According to the Government Accountability Office, the military has spent more than $200 million in the last ten years to replace personnel who were discharged for being openly gay. In 1998 twenty service members who could speak and translate Arabic, for example, were fired from their military positions because they were gay, despite a critical shortage of military personnel with important foreign language skills.

COMPELLED TO LIVE A LIE

Although the Don't Ask, Don't Tell policy was considered a compromise, it has come under fire from both gay rights advocates and opponents. Writer Tobias Wolff expresses an opinion that has been voiced often since the policy was enacted in 1993:

> Don't ask, don't tell is based on the precept that it is O.K. to admit gay service members and then compel them to live a lie. The military forces gay soldiers constantly to pretend that they are straight, not just with their peers but even with their parents, friends, and loved ones. The policy preserves no privacy or dignity for gay service members. It is a violation of our military's tradition of honor, integrity, and respect.

Homosexual members of the armed forces stage a 1993 rally in Washington, D.C., to demand an end to the military's anti–gay policies.

Quoted in Letters to the Editor, "For Gay Soldiers, Service Means Lying," *New York Times*, April 13, 1998, http://query.nytimes.com/gst/fullpage.html?res=940CEEDA113DF930A25757C0A96E958260.

State Workplace Rights for Gays and Lesbians

Though the federal government has been slow to make gay rights in the workplace a priority, some individual states have taken their own steps to promote the rights of gay workers. California is one of those states. In September 2004, California governor Arnold Schwarzenegger signed an assembly bill that required insurance companies to offer health, life, home owners, and auto insurance to registered domestic partners. Assemblywoman Christine Kehoe, an openly lesbian legislator from San Diego, sponsored the bill. Anticipating the January 2005 start of the domestic partnership law in California, Kehoe explains the need for passage of this bill: "This new law would

LEGISLATING MORALITY

Although many political conservatives oppose gays serving in the military under any circumstances, others strenuously disagree with this view. Republican Senator Barry Goldwater explained:

> The conservative movement, to which I subscribe, has as one of its basic tenets the belief that government should stay out of people's private lives. Government governs best when it governs least—and stays out of the impossible task of legislating morality. But legislating someone's version of morality is exactly what we do by perpetuating discrimination against gays.

> We can take polls. We can visit submarines to get opinions on who are the best citizens. But that is not the role of a democratic government in a free society. Under our Constitution, everyone is guaranteed the right to do as he pleases as long as it does not harm someone else. You don't need to be "straight" to fight and die for your country. You just need to shoot straight.

Quoted in Robert M. Baird and M. Katherine Baird, eds., *Homosexuality: Debating the Issues*. New York: Prometheus, 1995, p. 184.

protect families, eliminate uncertainty and confusion in current law and prevent unnecessary litigation."[50] Not everyone, however, applauded the bill's passage. Critics, including the Campaign for California Families and the Capitol Resource Institute, argued that it was not fair to force private businesses that were morally opposed to domestic partnerships to comply. They also argued that the bill's passage would cause health insurance costs to rise for California businesses.

Health insurance for partners of gay employees was at the heart of a ruling in December 2004 when the Montana Supreme Court ruled that its public universities must provide insurance coverage for the domestic part-

In 2004 a California attorney argues against the legality of granting same-sex couples the same legal rights as married heterosexual couples.

ners of gay employees. Gay rights advocates applauded the decision and viewed it as an important victory in a conservative state. In making the ruling, the court emphasized that gay marriage was not at issue, because one month earlier, Montana voters overwhelmingly voted to ban gay marriage in that state. Until the supreme court ruling, public universities in Montana limited health-care coverage to the children or married spouses of university employees. The court ruled that limiting health-care coverage in that way violated the equal protection clause of Montana's state constitution.

The one dissenting judge in the Montana case, Justice Jim Rice, disputed the claim that gay marriage was not an issue in the case. He claimed that promoting gay marriage was in fact at the heart of this case. He argued that the court's decision effectively diminished the status of marriage, making matrimony just another option without any exclusive legal benefits.

Rice explains his objection to the majority opinion: "This case is about the legal status of marriage in our society, specifically, whether the law still recognizes marriage as the transcendent societal relationship upon which government may base its decisions."[51] Rice expressed his belief that this decision, though it dealt directly with health insurance, was actually a roundabout way of attacking traditional marriage.

Gay Rights in the Private Sector

As cases such as those in Montana and California have slowly wound their way through courts and legislatures, progress for gay rights has moved more quickly in the private sector. Usually, minorities gain civil rights only after federal or state laws are passed to force private citizens or businesses to end discrimination. Racially integrating the public schools, for example, was accomplished only under great resistance after Congress passed civil rights legislation in the 1960s. In the fight for gay rights, however, private businesses have taken the initiative in the absence of such legislation. The first employer to offer domestic partner benefits to its gay employees was the *Village Voice*, a New York City weekly newspaper, which began its policy in 1982. The trend did not catch on quickly at first. By 1990 there were still fewer than two dozen employers who offered similar benefits. In 1992 the Lotus Development Corporation, now a division of IBM, became the first publicly traded company to offer domestic partnership benefits.

As the fight for gay rights in general has heated up, however, progress toward gay rights in the workplace has also picked up speed. The Human Rights Campaign (HRC), based in Washington, D.C., closely monitors gay

DISRUPTING LIVES

"Anti-gay discrimination can sap workplace productivity and disrupt the lives of people who simply want to do a good job, pay their taxes, and be responsible members of the community."

Massachusetts governor William Weld, quoted in Human Rights Campaign, "Nationwide Support for the Employment Non-Discrimination Act." www.hrc.org/Content/NavigationMenu/HRC/ Get_Informed/Federal_Legislation/Employment_ Non-Discrimination_Act/Background_Information/ Nationwide_Support_for_ENDA.htm.

A gay rights activist smiles as she holds Wal-Mart's 2003 announcement that the company's antidiscrimination policy had been expanded to protect homosexual employees.

rights in the workplace. When HRC released its third annual report card on corporate America's treatment of gay and lesbian employees in late September 2004, it announced that the number of companies that scored 100 percent doubled between 2003 and 2004. In fact, according to the report, 318 of the nation's 500 largest public employers now specifically ban discrimination based on sexual orientation. Human Rights Campaign has documented antidiscrimination policies that include sexual orientation at more than a thousand private companies nationwide.

One of the companies is in fact, Wal-Mart, the nation's largest public employer with 1.3 million workers in all fifty states. The company announced in 2003 that it had extended its antidiscrimination policy to include gay and lesbian workers. Shelley Alpern, the spokeswoman for the Equality Project, an advocacy group for gays in the workplace that had lobbied Wal-Mart to change its nondiscrimination policy, explains the importance of Wal-Mart's decision: "The significance almost can't be overstated.

They have a presence in all 50 states and also foreign countries, and the nation's largest private work force, and what they do sets an example for others in the retail industry. It will have a ripple effect."[52] Wal-Mart's decision both surprised and disappointed many conservatives who oppose such measures because they see them as counter to traditional family values, which have always been publicly embraced by Wal-Mart.

Many companies have even begun to offer benefits over and above the basics, both to retain and recruit gay employees and to remain competitive in the marketplace. Matt Murray of the *Wall Street Journal* explains how some large companies justify their gay-friendly policies: "[Companies] like Eli Lily [a large pharmaceutical company], have argued that adopting gay-friendly benefits is simply necessary to compete for talent in to-day's job market."[53] Many large companies consider it good business practice to do everything they can to retain highly trained employees and to pursue all investors, regardless of their sexual orientation. As being gay becomes more acceptable and more visible in society, businesses are also compelled to ac-tively pursue this growing segment of the marketplace and to maintain a gay-friendly image among the public at large.

Diversity at a Cost

However, the additional expense of offering domestic partner benefits presents a challenge for smaller companies. Though benefit policies at companies with fewer than fifty employees are not tracked in the same way as they are at larger companies, advocates on both sides of the issue acknowledge the difficulties that offering benefits to domestic partners present to small busi-nesses. The Corporate Resource Council, affiliated with the Al-liance Defense Fund, which opposes gay marriage, estimates that costs for employers could rise 3–5 percent even if only 1–2 percent of employees choose domestic partner benefits. It is also harder for small businesses to compensate for absent work-ers who take leave for health or child-care reasons, since extra employees are not always available to do additional work. Small businesses are in a much more precarious financial position than are large companies, which makes the balance between satisfying employees and customers and maintaining healthy profit margins more delicate.

Employees are not universally enthusiastic about the trend by large companies to include gays and lesbians in their nondiscrimination policies. In fact, a growing backlash by employees who see that trend as discriminatory toward their own conservative or religious views of homosexuality has become evident in recent years. Rolf Szabo, who had worked at the Eastman Kodak Company in Rochester, New York, for twenty-three years, was fired when he objected to an e-mail he received regarding the HRC's annual Coming Out Day. The e-mail message from Szabo's supervisor provided guidelines about what to say and how to act if another employee should happen to come out, or share information about his or her gay or lesbian sexual orientation. It was sent to one thousand Kodak employees. Szabo responded by sending this message of his own: "Please do not send this type of information to me anymore, as I find it disgusting and offensive."[54] Szabo was given the opportunity to apologize for his message, and when he refused, he was fired from the company.

Szabo's termination at Kodak for his antigay stance was widely publicized. Groups that promote gay rights applauded the action as a symbol of growing intolerance for antigay sentiment among big business. But religious conservatives and supporters of traditional family values criticized the firing as its own form of blatant discrimination. Bob Lonsberry, a talk show host in Rochester who raised the issue of Szabo's firing on his show, explained why the response to his show overwhelmingly favored Szabo's right to express his opinion: "In the name of tolerance

THE PRICE OF OPPOSING HOMOSEXUALITY

"It's a sad commentary on our times that today a person is probably more likely to be fired or disciplined at his job for *opposing* homosexuality than for being homosexual."

Peter J. LaBarbera, "Why a Gay Activist Columnist at the *Washington Times?*" Concerned Women for America, December 18, 2002. www.cwfa.org/articles/2942/CFI/cfreport/index.htm.

they foment a spirit of intolerance. Their ongoing incessant theme is diversity of the most progressive sort, but those in the workplace feel it's rubbed in their face."[55] Many of Szabo's fellow employees anonymously posted messages to the radio show, critical of the hypocrisy of Kodak's policies that forced them to hide their own opinions even as the company professed to promote diversity of all kinds.

When Secrets Are Revealed

Even though progress has been made in the last several years to combat overt discrimination against gays and lesbians in the workplace, there often remains a more subtle discrimination than, for example, outright insults by coworkers. In order to

In 2002 an attorney with the ACLU discusses a lawsuit her organization filed to represent an Alabama teacher who lost his job after his homosexuality was discovered.

survive the workplace and keep their jobs, gays and lesbians must often hide a huge part of their lives. They cannot talk about their relationships, or many of the day-to-day events that are regular topics of casual conversation at work. They often live with a pervasive sense of anxiety about revealing too much to the wrong person. In 1995 HRC began to collect personal stories from around the country to document this type of subtle workplace discrimination. The story of Ron Lambert, a warehouse overseer in Concord, New Hampshire, who was fired from his job in 1990, is typical of the HRC stories. Lambert, who had a reputation as an excellent employee, had received large bonuses and much praise for reducing costs and increasing business. As he became friendly with his coworkers and began spending time with their families, Lambert revealed his homosexuality privately to some of these coworkers. Unexpectedly, he was told that he was "not the man for the job"[56] and fired. He was given no explanation for his sudden firing, but a fellow manager confirmed his suspicion that he was fired because he was gay.

A similar case occurred in Alabama when graduate student John Howard lost his job giving tours of a regional paper company's private art collection in the early 1990s. Howard was president of the University of Alabama's Gay and Lesbian Alliance. When another employee told the supervisor that Howard was gay, he was called into the office and asked outright whether he was gay and whether he belonged to any gay organizations. When Howard acknowledged that he was both gay and belonged to the Gay and Lesbian Alliance, he was told that although his work was excellent, his sexual orientation was a problem, and he was fired. These two cases are among hundreds that were collected by HRC to illustrate the undercurrent of discrimination that exists for gay and lesbian employees in the workplace.

A Different Twist

Though most cases of discrimination for sexual orientation target gays and lesbians, in one case an employee was fired because she was not gay. Carolyn O'Neill, a single mother of three children, was a waitress at a bar in Tampa, Florida, in 1993, when the bar's owners decided to change its focus and market primarily to gay and lesbian customers. They fired all their heterosexual employees and hired a new staff consisting only of gay men. When the gay and lesbian community learned about the firings, they staged a boycott of the bar to protest the discrimination. The boycott was successful, and the bar went out of business. According to the report in the HRC's Documenting Discrimination project, one of the boycott leaders observes, "Sexual orientation has no bearing on your capacity to mix drinks. Discrimination is wrong whether it's directed against gays and lesbians or straights."[57]

Ongoing Battles

As gays and lesbians and their supporters plan strategies to continue to bring progress through the gay rights movement, they wrestle with questions concerning comfort levels and how to move forward without provoking a backlash from conservatives. The country is far from united on the issue of gay rights. Gay rights advocates continue to wage battles for legal acceptance of their families and relationships and for benefits in the workplace. At the same time, religious and political conservatives continue to argue that homosexuality is wrong and should not be officially recognized and protected with laws and benefits. They choose specific political battles with the goal of motivating passage of a constitutional amendment that would forever outlaw gay marriage.

Many gay rights advocates draw parallels between the pace of change for gay rights and the civil rights movement forty years ago. Ellen Goodman, a columnist for the *Boston Globe*, frames the question: "Do you wait for people to be more comfortable to make change? Or do people only become more comfortable in the wake of change?"[58] There was a time when the idea of integrated schools and recreation facilities seemed outrageous. And now children born in the 1990s can barely fathom the idea that once everyone was not allowed to drink from the same water fountain. Time will tell whether gay rights will follow a similar path.

Chapter 1

1. The author explains that police raids at the Stonewall Inn in New York City were not uncommon. What factors led patrons to fight back on the days known as the Stonewall rebellion?

2. Why did homosexual activists believe that it was important to convince psychiatrists that homosexuality was not a mental disorder?

3. How do many conservative groups, including Citizens for Community Values, explain their belief that some traditions, including family structure, can never change?

Chapter 2

1. Both advocates and opponents of gay marriage have argued against alternatives such as gay unions and domestic partnerships. What are their reasons and how do they differ?

2. Supporters of California's Propositon 22, which restricted marriage to one man and one woman, said the state should protect opposite-sex marriage to encourage procreation. When Judge Richard Kramer overturned Prop 22, he said that having children is not necessarily the purpose of marriage. How does each side support its argument?

3. Why do some people believe that it is wrong to compare bans on gay marriage to bans on interracial marriage?

Chapter 3

1. According to the author, scientists have not found a so-called gay gene. How would the existence or nonexistence of a gay gene affect the argument about whether being raised in a gay household is harmful to children?

2. Why do some people think it is wrong to study how children turn out when they are raised in gay families? Do you agree? Why or why not?

3. How do child custody decisions after a divorce reflect society's mixed attitudes toward gay parents?

Chapter 4

1. According to the 2001 publication *Hatred in the Hallways*, what uncomfortable or discriminatory situations do gay and lesbian students face in school?

2. Should schools teach tolerance toward gays and lesbians? Support your position with arguments by parents, teachers, and students.

3. Why do some people believe that Harvey Milk High School does not serve the best interests of either straight or homosexual students?

Chapter 5

1. The author explains how Wal-Mart changed its policy regarding gay workers. Why is Wal-Mart's position on antidiscrimination considered so important?

2. How has the Don't ask, Don't tell policy affected people who serve in the U.S. military?

3. What potential positive and negative effects could domestic partnership benefits have on small businesses?

NOTES

Chapter 1: A New Civil Rights Movement

1. Martin Duberman, *Cures*. New York: Dutton, 1991, pp. 158–59.
2. Duberman, *Cures*, p. 161.
3. Ronald Bayer, *Homosexuality and American Psychiatry*. New York: Basic Books, 1981, p. 97.
4. Quoted in Alix Spiegel, "81 Words," *This American Life*, Chicago Public Radio, January 18, 2002.
5. Quoted in Spiegel, "81 Words."
6. Quoted in Bayer, *Homosexuality and American Psychiatry*, p. 138.
7. Citizens for Community Values, "The Homosexual Issue: Where Do We Stand and Why?" www.ccv.org/Homosexuality-Where_CCV_Stands.htm.
8. CCV, "The Homosexual Issue."
9. Abigail Garner, *Families Like Mine*. New York: Harper-Collins, 2004, p. 127.
10. Religious Tolerance.org, "Professional Associations' Statements About Homosexuality." http://religioustolerance.org/hom_prof.htm.
11. Religious Tolerance.org, "Changing Gays and Lesbians: Ex-Gay and Transformational Ministries." http://religioustolerance.org/hom_evan.htm.
12. Quoted in Religious Tolerance.org, "Changing Gays and Lesbians."

Chapter 2: Gay Marriage

13. Greg Moran, "Marriage's Myriad Privileges Key in Same-Sex Union Debate," *San Diego Union-Tribune*, March 21, 2004, p. A19.

14. Troy D. Perry, "Why I Believe in Marriage Equality," *San Diego Union-Tribune*, March 14, 2004, p. G4.

15. Robert Benne and Gerald McDermott, "Speaking Out: Why Gay Marriage Would Be Harmful," *Christianity Today.com.* February 19, 2004. www.christianitytoday.com/ct/2004/107/ 41.0.html.

16. Jonathan Rauch, *Gay Marriage: Why It Is Good for Gays, Good for Straights, and Good for America.* New York: Henry Holt, 2004, p. 125.

17. Quoted in Lisa Leff, "Judge Annuls Ban on Gay Nuptials," *San Diego Union-Tribune*, March 15, 2005, p. A11.

18. Rauch, *Gay Marriage*, p. 24.

19. Benne and McDermott, "Speaking Out."

20. Quoted in Tony Perkins, "Preserving Marriage, Saving Society," *San Diego Union-Tribune*, March 14, 2004, p. G1.

21. Perkins, "Preserving Marriage, Saving Society."

22. Quoted in Stephen Dinan, "Bush Vows to Defend Sanctity of Marriage," *Washington Times*, November 19, 2003. www.washingtontimes.com/national/20031118-113126-473r.htm.

23. Quoted in Leff, "Judge Annuls Ban on Gay Nuptials."

24. Quoted in Stephen Henderson, "Gay-Rights Activists Press Their Case for Marriage in New Jersey," Human Rights Campaign, December 8, 2004. www.hrc.org/Content/Content Groups/News3/2004_December/Gay-Rights_Activists_Press_ Their_Case_for_Marriage_in_New_Jersey.htm.

25. *New York Times*, "The Road to Gay Marriage," March 7, 2004, p. 12.

Chapter 3: Gay Families

26. Susan Dominus, "Growing Up with Mom and Mom," *New York Times Magazine*, October 24, 2004, p. 70.

27. Suzanne M. Johnson and Elizabeth O'Connor, *The Gay Baby Boom*. New York: New York University Press, 2002, p. 53.

28. American College of Pediatricians, "Homosexual Parenting: Is It Time for Change?" January 22, 2004. http://acpeds.org/? CONTEXT=art&cat=10005&art=50&BISKIT=924484903.

29. Benedict Carey, "Experts Dispute Bush on Gay-Adoption Issue," *New York Times*, January 29, 2005, p. A12.

30. Quoted in Garner, *Families Like Mine*, p. 19.

31. Quoted in Kristen Kreisher, "Gay Adoption," Child Welfare League of America, January 2002. www.cwla.org/articles/cv0201gayadopt.htm.

32. Quoted in Lynn Waddell, "Gays in Florida Seek Adoption Alternatives," *New York Times*, January 21, 2005, p. A21.

33. Quoted in Kreisher, "Gay Adoption."

34. Oregon Defense of Marriage Coalition, "Questions and Answers About Measure 36." www.defenseofmarriagecoalition.org/gaymarriageqa.php.

35. David Kravets, "Biological Mother Loses Custody Case," *San Diego Union-Tribune*, May 12, 2004, p. A3.

Chapter 4: Gay Rights in Schools

36. Human Rights Watch, *Hatred in the Hallways*, 2001. www.hrw.org/reports/2001/uslgbt/Final-02.htm.

37. National Association for Research and Therapy of Homosexuality, "New York Gay Rights Bill Targets Schools," September 19, 2004. www.narth.com/docs/targets.html.

38. American Civil Liberties Union, "Federal Appeals Court Says Schools Must Protect Gay Students from Harassment," April 8, 2003. http://aclunc.org/pressrel/030409-flores.html.

39. Tom Owens, "Same-Sex Prom Dates: The Right to Dance," Tolerance.org, April 21, 2005. www.tolerance.org/teens/stories/article.jsp?p=0&ar=139.

40. Quoted in the Family Foundation of Kentucky, "Alliance Defense Fund Assists Parents Chafing Under School 'Gay Tolerance' Training," May/June 2005. www.tffky.org/articles/2005/200505d.html.

41. Citizens for Community Values, "'The Homosexual Issue': Where Do We Stand and Why?" www.ccv.org/Homosexuality-Where_CCV_Stands.htm.

42. Quoted in Art McFarland, "Gay Public High School to Open

Doors This Fall," July 28, 2003. 7online.com. abclocal.go.com/wabc/news/wabc_072803_gayschool.html.

43. Quoted in John Colapinto, "The Harvey Milk High School Has No Right to Exist. Discuss." *New York Magazine* online, February 7, 2005. www.newyorkmetro.com/nymetro/news/features/10970/index.html.

44. Quoted in Colapinto, "The Harvey Milk School Has No Right to Exist. Discuss."

45. Quoted in Tamar Lewin, "Battle on Gay Pride Shirts Leads to Suit Against School," *New York Times*, November 24, 2004, p. A16.

46. Quoted in Onell R. Soto, "Judge Says Ruling Ahead in Anti-Gay T-Shirt Case," *San Diego Union-Tribune*, September 17, 2004, p. B1.

Chapter 5: Gay Rights in the Workplace

47. Quoted in Human Rights Campaign, "National Support for the Non-Discrimination Act." www.hrc.org/Content/Navigation Menu/HRC/Get_Informed/Federal_Legislation/Employment _Non-Discrimination_Act/Background_Information/Nation wide_Support_for_ENDA.htm.

48. Quoted in John Files, "Number of Gays Discharged from Services Drops Again," *New York Times*, February 13, 2005, p. 21.

49. Quoted in Files, "Number of Gays Discharged from Services Drops Again."

50. Quoted in Bill Ainsworth, "Governor Signs First Major Gay Rights Bill," *San Diego Union-Tribune*, September 14, 2004, p. A3.

51. Quoted in Adam Liptak, "Montana Universities Must Offer Health Insurance to Gay Employees' Partners, Court Rules," *New York Times*, December 31, 2004, p. A18.

52. Quoted in Matt Murray, "Shift Shows Acceptance of Gay Professionals," CareerJournal.com, July 22, 2003. www.career journal.com/myc/diversity/20030722-murray.html.

53. Murray, "Shift Shows Acceptance of Gay Professionals."

54. Quoted in WorldNetDaily, "Kodak Fires Man over 'Gay' Stance," October 24, 2002. www.worldnetdaily.com/news/ article.asp?ARTICLE_ID=29394.

55. Quoted in WorldNetDaily, "Kodak Fires Man over 'Gay' Stance."

56. Quoted in Human Rights Campaign, "Stellar Worker Fired from New Hampshire Warehouse Job." www.hrc.org/Tem plate.cfm?Section=Documenting_Discrimination1&Template =/ContentManagement/ContentDisplay.cfm&ContentID=111 36.

57. Quoted in Human Rights Campaign, "Tampa Bartender Replaced Because She Is Not Gay." www.hrc.org/Template.cfm? Section=Documenting_Discrimination1&Template=/Content Management/ContentDisplay.cfm&ContentID=11138.

58. Ellen Goodman, "Must Gay Rights Wait for Our 'Comfort'?" *Boston Globe*, December 16, 2004. www.boston.com/news/ globe/editorial_opinion/oped/articles/2004/12/16/must_gay _rights_wait_ for_our_comfort.

ORGANIZATIONS TO CONTACT

Children of Lesbians and Gays Everywhere (COLAGE)

3543 Eighteenth St., #1, San Francisco, CA 94110

(415) 861-5437

www.colage.org

COLAGE is a support organization for children of gay, lesbian, bisexual, and transgender parents. The Web site includes an online newsletter.

Concerned Women for America

1015 Fifteenth St. NW, Suite 1100, Washington, DC 20005

phone: (202) 488-7000

fax: (202) 488-0806

www.cwfa.org

This organization claims to be the largest public policy women's organization in the country whose mission is to promote and protect biblical values among all citizens. It focuses on issues that can be addressed through prayer, education, and advocacy, and works to restore the family to its original purpose.

Family Research Council

801 G St. NW, Washington, DC 20001

phone: (202) 393-2100

fax: (202) 393-2134

www.frc.org

This conservative organization operates on the principle that marriage and family is the basis of civilization and society. It champions the Judeo-Christian worldview that God is the author of life, liberty, and the family, and often supports legislation and public policy that conform to these values.

Gay and Lesbian Alliance Against Defamation (GLAAD)

248 West Thirty-fifth St., Eighth Floor, New York, NY 10001

(212) 629-3322

www.glaad.org

GLAAD's mission is to make sure that the media portray gays and lesbians in fair and accurate ways.

Hetrick-Martin Institute (Home of Harvey Milk High School)

2 Astor Place, New York, NY, 10003
phone: (212) 674-2400
fax: (212) 674-8650
www.hmi.org

Hetrick-Martin Institute, which founded Harvey Milk High School in New York City, is the oldest and largest nonprofit agency created to serve gay and lesbian youth between the ages of twelve and twenty-one.

Institute for American Values

1841 Broadway, Suite 211, New York, NY 10023
(212) 246-3942
www.americanvalues.org

This private, nonpartisan organization describes its mission as one of devotion to marriage and family life, and to opening up discussion about traditional values versus change in American culture.

Parents, Families and Friends of Lesbians and Gays (PFLAG)

1726 M St. NW, Suite 400, Washington, DC 20036
(202) 467-8180
www.pflag.org

This is a support and advocacy organization with chapters across the United States and around the world. It is particularly useful for advising gay and lesbian teens about dealing with their families.

Women's Educational Media

2180 Bryant St., Suite 203, San Francisco, CA 94110
phone: (415) 641-4616
fax: (415) 641-4632
www.womedia.org

This group produces and directs films, and creates educational resources to lobby for social change. Their film *Choosing Children* chronicles gay adoption; *One Wedding and a Revolution* documents the 4,000 same-sex marriages that took place in San Francisco in 2004. *It's Elementary: Talking About Gay Issues in Schools* guides educators in the discussion of gay families.

FOR MORE INFORMATION

Books

Tricia Andryszewski, *Gay Rights*. Brookfield, CT: Twenty-First Century, 2000. Traces the history of the gay rights movement in America, from the Stonewall riots to the turn of the twenty-first century.

Kate Burns, ed., *Gay Marriage*. San Diego: Greenhaven, 2004. Presents all perspectives of the debate about gay marriage.

Martin Duberman, *Cures: A Gay Man's Odyssey*. New York: Dutton, 1991. A distinguished history professor's memoir of his life as a gay man and his attempt to find a cure for his homosexuality in an era when homosexuality was considered an illness.

Robert E. Dunbar, *Homosexuality*. Springfield, NJ: Enslow, 1995. Discusses various perspectives on the topic, including scientific and religious viewpoints and legal issues.

Abigail Garner, *Families Like Mine*. New York: HarperCollins, 2004. The author, the daughter of a gay man, sympathetically explores the lives of many gay families and discusses the support systems that are available for children of gay parents. Includes an extensive list of resources.

Eric Marcus, *What If Someone I Know Is Gay? Answers to Questions About Gay and Lesbian People*. New York: Price Stern Sloan, 2000. Written in a reader-friendly question-and-answer style, this book has chapters that address the major questions concerning gay teens and their straight peers. Questions range from basic (What does gay mean?) to complex (addressing dating, religion, and dealing with gay issues in school). Includes an extensive list of resources: helpful and supportive Web sites, books, organizations, and videos.

Marilyn Tower Oliver, *Gay and Lesbian Rights: A Struggle*. Springfield, NJ: Enslow, 1998. Examines the history of the gay rights movement in the United States and arguments both for and against gay rights.

Janice E. Rench, *Understanding Sexual Identity: A Book for Gay Teens and Their Friends*. Minneapolis: Lerner, 1990. This informative book, in question-and-answer format, is supportive of gay and lesbian teens. Each chapter begins with an anecdote about a gay or lesbian teen in need of support or information, and then addresses the questions raised by the anecdote.

Diane Silver, *The New Civil War: The Lesbian and Gay Struggle for Civil Rights*. New York: Franklin Watts, 1997. Describes the struggles by American gays and lesbians to obtain equal rights.

Mary Williams, *Opposing Viewpoints: Homosexuality*. San Diego: Greenhaven, 1991. Presents all sides of the debate about homosexuality, whether its origin is biological or freely chosen as well as many other aspects of this topic.

Periodicals

Susan Dominus, "Growing Up with Mom and Mom," *New York Times Magazine*, October 24, 2004.

Tony Perkins, "Preserving Marriage, Saving Society," *San Diego Union-Tribune*, March 14, 2004.

Troy D. Perry, "Why I Believe in Marriage Equality," *San Diego Union-Tribune*, March 14, 2004.

Jack Thomas, "Not Better, Not Worse, Just Different," *San Diego Union-Tribune*, June 13, 2004.

Internet Sources

Human Rights Campaign, "Documenting Discrimination Project." www.hrc.org/Template.cfm?Section=Documenting-Discrimination 1&Template=/ContentManagement/Content Display.cfm &ContentID=11134.

Human Rights Watch, *Hatred in the Hallways*, 2001. www.hrw.org/reports/2001/uslgbt/Final-02.htm.

Web Sites

Alliance Defense Fund (www.alliancedefensefund.org). This Christian legal advocacy group works to defend religious freedom. They support the rights of students and others to express views in support of traditional marriage, and the right for their opinions to be voiced in the schools.

Children of Lesbians and Gays Everywhere (COLAGE) (www.colage.org). COLAGE works to support and represent the children of gay, lesbian, bisexual, and transgender parents. The Web site includes an online newsletter and resources for both gay and straight teens.

Gay, Lesbian, and Straight Education Network (GLSEN) (www.glsen.org). GLSEN works to make sure that gay and lesbian students are protected and valued in school communities, and promotes gay-straight alliances in schools across the country. The Web site has extensive resources for teachers and students.

Human Rights Campaign (www.hrc.org). The Human Rights Campaign is the largest gay, lesbian, transgender, and bisexual advocacy organization in the United States. Its comprehensive site offers articles and information about the history of gay rights and current legislative lobbying efforts.

Human Rights Watch (www.hrw.org). Human Rights Watch is an international nongovernmental human rights organization whose mission is to protect all groups of people and expose human rights violations. Its Web site includes a section devoted to LGBT (lesbian, gay, bisexual, and transgender) rights, with links to international news stories, reports, and government resolutions, and films and other Web resources about gay rights.

Liberty Counsel (www.lc.org). This nationwide nonprofit organization based in Orlando, Florida, is dedicated to advancing religious freedom, the sanctity of human life, and the traditional family. It opposes same-sex marriage and same-sex adoption, and its Web site offers statistics and commentary to support its position.

Student Pride USA (www.studentprideUSA.org). This project is run by students across the United States to provide materials, education, and communication for gay-straight alliances in the schools.

Video and DVD

Debra Chasnoff and Helen Cohen, viewing guide for *It's Elementary: Talking About Gay Issues in Schools*. San Francisco: Women's Educational Media, 1997. This video guides educators in discussing gay families with young children.

Murray Nossel, *Paternal Instinct*, 2003. (www.paternalinstinct film.com/paternal.swf). The film chronicles a gay couple's successful efforts to become biological parents, from placing an ad for a surrogate mother on the Internet to fathering two daughters through surrogacy within three years.

Tom Shepard, *Scout's Honor*, 2001. (www.scouts-honor.com). A documentary aired on PBS, tracing the conflict between the antigay policies of the Boy Scouts of America and the efforts by many of its members to overturn those policies. The story is told from the points of view of a thirteen-year-old boy and a seventy-year-old man.

Alix Spiegel, "81 Words," *This American Life*, episode 204, *WBEZ*, Chicago Public Radio, January 18, 2002. This radio magazine tells the story of the American Psychiatric Association's reclassification and removal of homosexuality from its list of mental disorders in 1973.

Johnny Symons, *Daddy & Papa*, New York, 2002. (www.daddy andpapa.com). Award-winning documentary about four gay families and their battles to gain legal status.

INDEX

PICTURE CREDITS

Cover photo: © Christine Schneider/zefa/CORBIS

AP/Wide World Photos, 13, 36, 41, 47, 54, 57, 60, 62, 65, 72, 77, 79, 82

© Bettmann/CORBIS, 19

© Cam Cardow/The Ottawa Citizen/Cagle Cartoons. All rights reserved, 22

© Jeff Christensen/Reuters/CORBIS, 67

Porter Gifford/Getty Images News/Getty Images, 75

© Mimmo Jodice/CORBIS, 9

© Nancy Kaszerman/ZUMA/CORBIS, 7

© Mike Keefe/The Denver Post/Cagle Cartoons. All rights reserved, 33

© Frederic Larson/San Francisco Chronicle/CORBIS, 30

© Jeff Parker/Florida Today/Cagle Cartoons. All rights reserved, 51

© Monte Wolverton/Cagle Cartoons. All rights reserved, 35

Alex Wong/Getty Images News/Getty Images, 25

Taro Yamasaki/Time Life Pictures/Getty Images, 46

Steve Zmina, 10, 28, 39, 43, 52

ABOUT THE AUTHOR

Tina Kafka teaches science and is the curriculum coordinator at Explorer Elementary Charter School in San Diego, California. She also wrote *DNA on Trial* published by Lucent Books, which won the San Diego Book Award for Children's and Young Adult's Nonfiction in 2004. She and her husband, who is also a teacher and a woodworker, enjoy keeping up with their 1911 house, visiting their three children who live in New York City, and traveling during the summers.